BEGIN TO KNIT

LECTOR HOUSE PUBLIC DOMAIN WORKS

BEGIN TO KNIT

ANONYMOUS

ISBN: 978-93-90314-11-9

Published: -

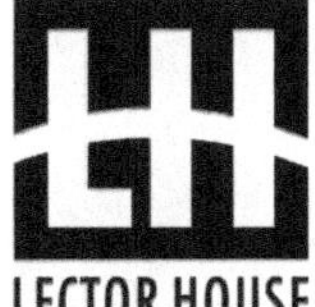

LECTOR HOUSE LLP
E-MAIL: lectorpublishing@gmail.com

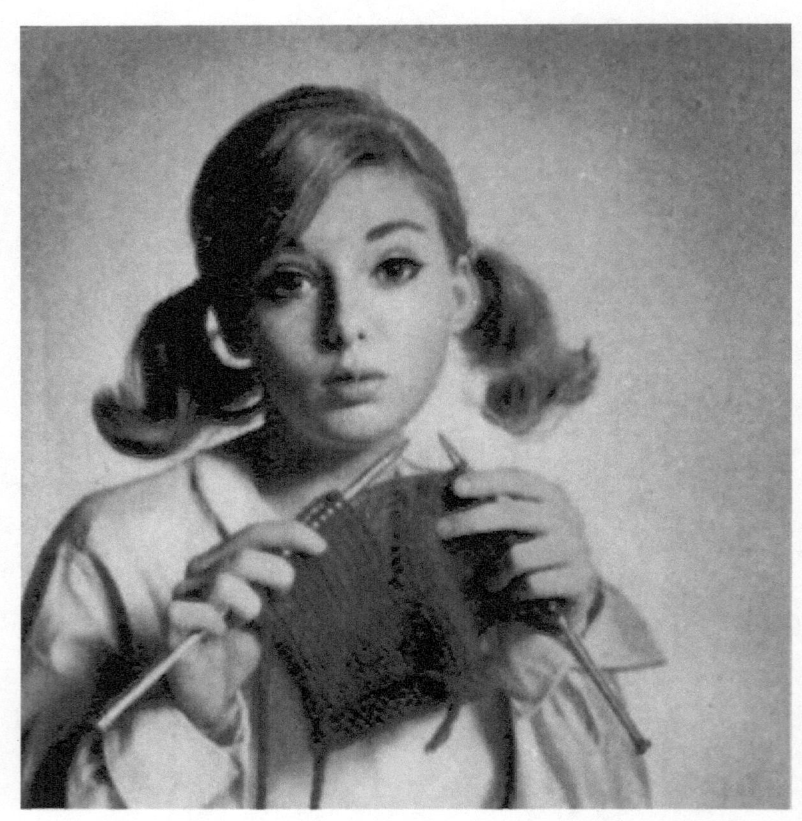

SO!

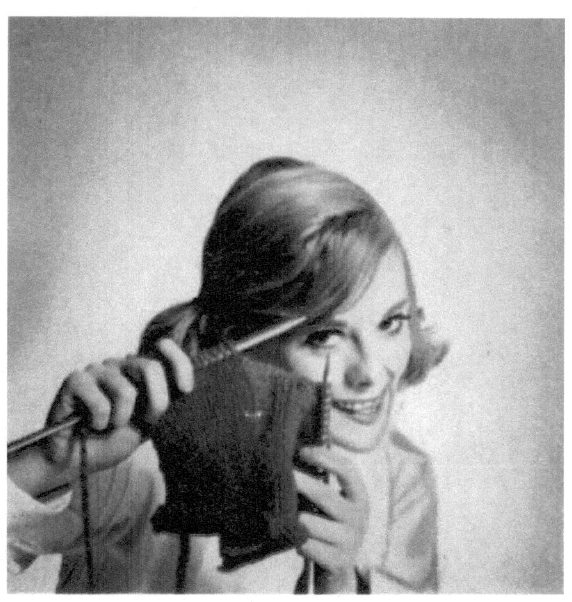

YOU WANT TO KNIT?

Well, why not when it's so easy with DAWN yarns and this easy-to-follow instruction book. You'll find plain and fancy stitches and difficult looking but oh, so easy to knit designs. And when these designs are knitted with the soft pastels or bright, gay colors of DAWN Yarns ... Zowie, you're in!

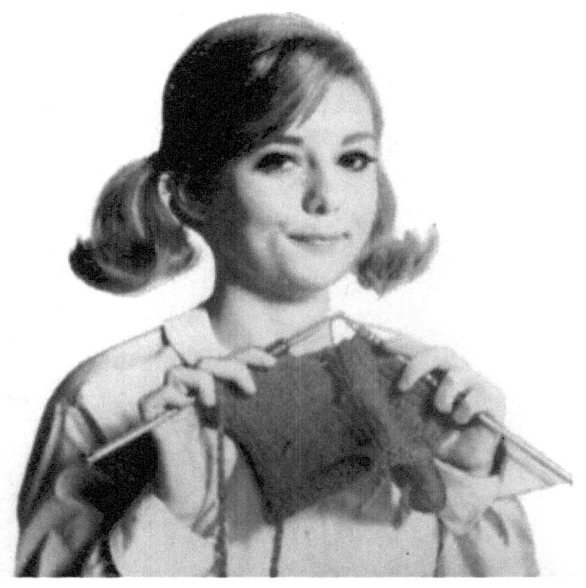

AMERICAN THREAD CO.
STAR BOOK NO. 201

BEGIN TO KNIT

ALL THE BASIC STITCHES • EASY NOVELTY STITCHES • QUICK THINGS TO MAKE

BY

ANONYMOUS

CONTENTS

Page

I. BASIC NEEDS AND KNOW HOW..... 1
- FUNDAMENTALS & SOME TIPS 1
- WINDING WOOL 1
- NEEDLE TYPES. 2
- CASTING ON 3
- PLAIN KNITTING 5
- GARTER STITCH. 6
- PURLING 7
- STOCKINETTE STITCH 8
- RIBBING 9
- TO DECREASE OR NARROW 10
- PASS SLIP STITCH OVER (P.S.S.O.) 10
- TO INCREASE 12
- YARN OVER.... 13
- BIND OFF 14
- TO SLIP A STITCH..... .16
- PICKING UP STITCHES .... DROPPED ST 16
- PICKING UP STITCHES 17
- BUTTONHOLES 17
- WEAVING TOE 18
- DUPLICATE STITCH 19
- CHANGING COLORS.... .20
- GENERAL INFORMATION. 21
- CHANGING SIZES. 21

- CHILD'S OR IN-BETWEEN SIZE. 21
- BLOCKING AND FINISHING 22
- TO SHORTEN 23
- TO LENGTHEN 24

II. SNUG AND COMFORTABLE ... AND EASY TO MAKE 25
- KNITTED AFGHAN SIZE: 48 × 60 INCHES. 25

III. FIVE FANCY STITCHES—LOOK HARD TO DO—BUT EASY TO MAKE. 27
- PATTERN NO. 1 27
- PATTERN NO. 2 28
- PATTERN NO. 3 29
- PATTERN NO. 4 30
- PATTERN NO. 5 31

IV. PLAIN SOCKS FOR A GO-GO GUY 32
- MEN'S SHORT SOCKS 33

V. DOLLS AND GUYS TWO NEEDLE MITTENS 34

VI. FOR THE YEARLING ... THE SWEATER. 36
- SIZE: 6 MONTHS TO 1 YEAR. 36
- SWEATER 36

VII. ... AND EASY TO MAKE HAT BOOTIES AND MITTENS 38
- BOOTIES. 38
- MITTENS 39
- HAT 39

VIII. HAPPY SWEATER DATES 41
- HIS SLIPOVER SIZES: 40, 42 AND 44 41
- HER RAGLAN SIZES: SMALL, MEDIUM AND LARGE 42
- BASIC CROCHET 43

IX. CLAM DIGGERS SHELL. 44
- SIZES: SMALL, MEDIUM, LARGE 44

X. POM PON PONCHO 46

- SIZE: ONE SIZE FITS ALL 46

XI. PRETEEN SLIPOVER 48
- SIZES 4, 6, 8, 10, 12, 14 48

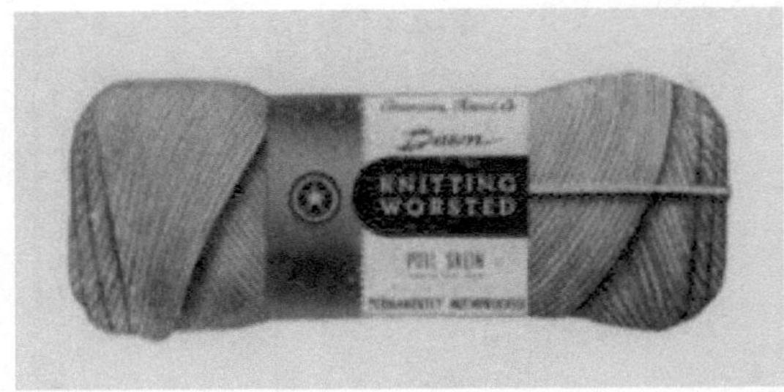

TALK OF THE TRADE

ABBREVIATIONS

K	Knit
P	Purl
St(s)	Stitch(es)
YO	Yarn Over
Dec.	Decrease
Inc.	Increase
Tog.	Together
Rnd.	Round
P.s.s.o.	Pass slip st over st
dpn	Double pointed needle
K-O	Do not work st, row or round
Beg.	Beginning
Bet.	Between
*	an asterisk. This indicates that the instructions following are to be repeated across row or for the number of stitches or times specified.

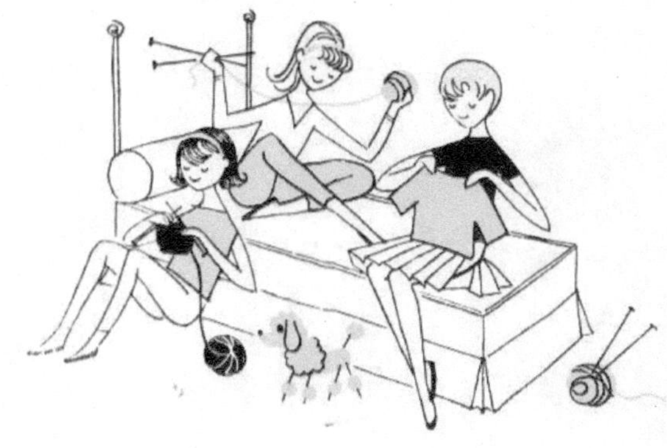

BASIC NEEDS AND KNOW HOW....

YARNS: Yarns vary in size, twist and texture. Use the "**Dawn**" Yarn indicated in the directions as only an experienced expert knitter knows how to allow for the difference when a substitution is made. It is also very important to purchase all the yarn needed at one time as different dye lots frequently have different shades of color.

When you purchase your yarn always check the dye lot number to make certain they are all the same. It is much wiser to purchase a little extra yarn than to try and match the dye lot after your garment is finished. Though the color may look the same in the skein more often than not the difference will be seen in the finished work. The "ply" of yarn means the number of strands twisted together. This can be seen by taking the end of the yarn and untwisting.

FUNDAMENTALS & SOME TIPS

Learn the basic stitches. There are only three: Knit, Purl and slip. All the others are produced by variations and in combination with yarn overs. See page 10.

Practice first with heavy yarn and thick needles. Study the stitch and the position it takes on the needle. Follow arrows in illustration. Learn to recognize when it is wrong. Watch the yarn to see where each loop of the stitch begins and ends. If you lay your knitting aside for a few days or longer, always rip back a few rows before starting again. This will prevent an uneven row. See page 12 for ripping back.

Parentheses in our instructions are used for an explanation of a st, a certain section of a garment, or change of sts for change of size. A **ROW** is once across the needle. A **RIDGE** is 2 rows, back and forth. **WORK EVEN**, means to continue in pattern st keeping the continuity of the design.

Always **MEASURE** straight up and down unless otherwise stated.

WINDING WOOL

Winding the wool correctly is important. Never wind wool tightly as this stretches it. Wind several strands around fingers, slip these from fingers. Over these strands, in opposite direction, wind a few more strands wrapping yarn around fingers and ball. Continue in this manner, always winding over fingers and in opposite direction from last winding.

LEFT HAND KNITTING: Follow the instructions but change your copy to read left hand where it says "right hand" and vice versa. Use a mirror to study diagrams and charts. This will reverse the image for you.

JOINING YARNS ... If possible, join the new yarn with a knot at the beginning of a row. If this cannot be done, work next st with new yarn leaving a 4 inch length. Work a few sts, tie the ends firmly and with a yarn needle weave ends into work.

MARKER ... This term is used whenever it is important that a certain point is to be marked. Example: increase, decrease, beginning of a row or round, buttonholes, center st, etc. To make a marker of yarn, use a different color; make a slip knot leaving ends about 2 inches in length. Place on needle as directed. Slip marker off one needle to the other needle in each successive round.

MULTIPLE OF STS ... This term is used generally at beginning of directions and means that a certain multiple of sts is necessary to work one pattern. Example: multiple of 4 sts would mean any number divisible by 4 or 12, 16, 24 sts, etc. A multiple of 4 plus 2 would be 14, 18, 26 sts, etc., or any number that has 2 more sts after dividing by 4.

NEEDLE TYPES

STRAIGHT NEEDLES ... are used when working back and forth in rows. They come in lengths of 10, 12, and 14 inches and sizes O-1-2-3, etc. The larger the number, the thicker the needle.

DOUBLE POINTED NEEDLES ... come in sets of 4 or 5. They are used for socks, mittens and any articles made in rounds.

CIRCULAR NEEDLES ... are used in making skirts, or parts of garments when a seam is not desired; also in completing a large doily or a round tablecloth.

Directions give the size and type needle required and it is not advisable to change the size unless it is necessary in order to obtain the correct gauge.

CABLE NEEDLES ... are short with a bend in the center to hold sts from slipping off. They are available in thin or thick size for the different yarns. A short double pointed needle may also be used. It is a good idea after placing sts on the straight needle to be used for cable to stick needle into garment slightly, this will prevent sts from slipping off needle.

STITCH HOLDERS ... are used to hold sts to be used later. Example: sts at back of neck or when all sts are cast on and worked to armholes, then divided for front and back. The stitch holders can be purchased or a safety pin or length of yarn may be used.

STITCH COUNTERS ... usually placed on knitting needles. They have a dial and after working a row, turn the dial to the next number.

BOBBINS ... usually made of plastic to hold small amounts of yarn for use in making argyle socks or the Fair Isle, Scandinavian or Ski patterns.

GAUGE ... The stitch gauge which appears at the beginning of all instructions is most important to the size and fit of your garment. Before starting, make a sample swatch of the pattern stitch with the needles and yarn specified. If you have

MORE sts than gauge use LARGER needles. If you have LESS sts than gauge use SMALLER needles. Check your gauge as you progress to assure a perfectly sized garment, Ill. No. 1.

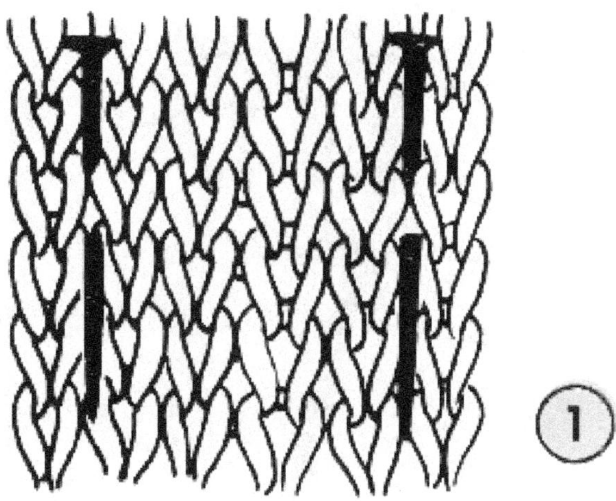

CASTING ON

Allow about ½ inch for each st for fine yarn and 1 inch for each st for heavy yarn. Make a slip knot on needle, Ill. No. 2. * Hold needle in right hand, hold both lengths of yarn in left hand (see arrows) having short end of yarn under and to outside of thumb and main length of yarn under and to outside of forefinger, Ill. No. 3. Insert needle through loop formed on thumb, pick up yarn on forefinger and draw through loop, Ill. No. 4, let loop drop from thumb and tighten st on right needle with thumb. Repeat from * leaving about ¼ inch between sts until required number of sts have been cast on, Ill. No. 5.

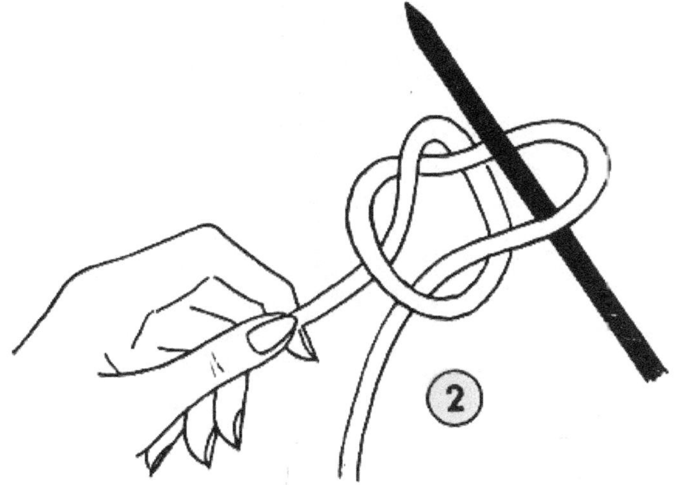

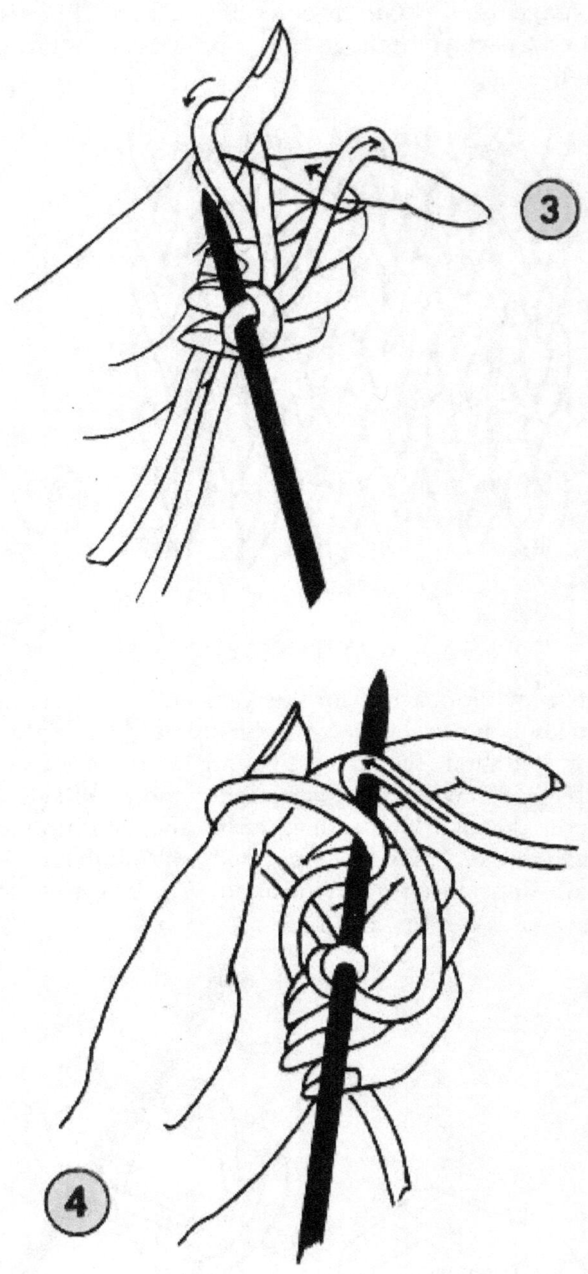

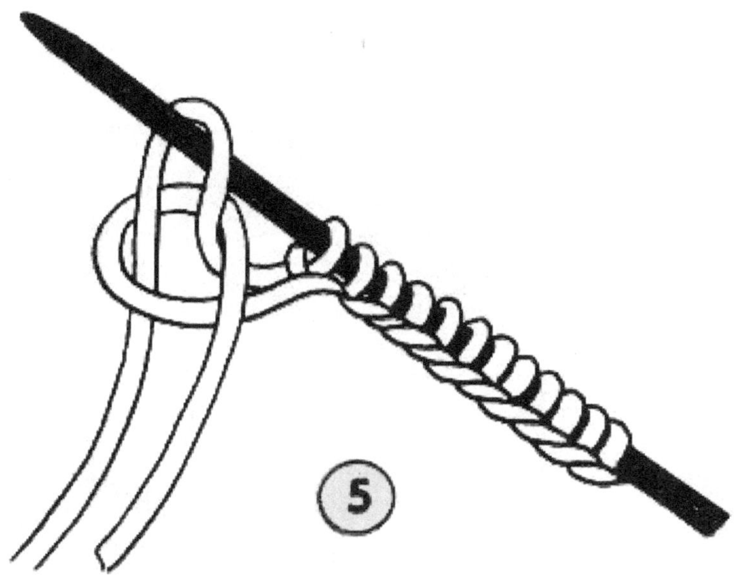

PLAIN KNITTING

Hold needle containing stitches in left hand. Follow arrows. * With yarn in back of work, insert free needle from left to right in front of st, yarn under and over point of needle and draw through st, slip stitch just worked from left needle. Retain new stitch on right needle. Repeat from * until all stitches are on right needle. **2nd Row and Succeeding Rows**: Place the needle holding stitches in left hand with free needle in right hand. Insert free needle in 1st stitch and complete same as 1st row.

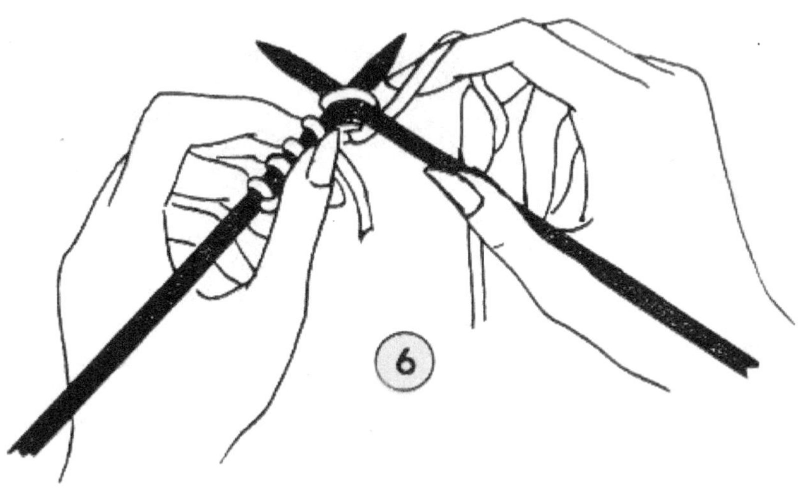

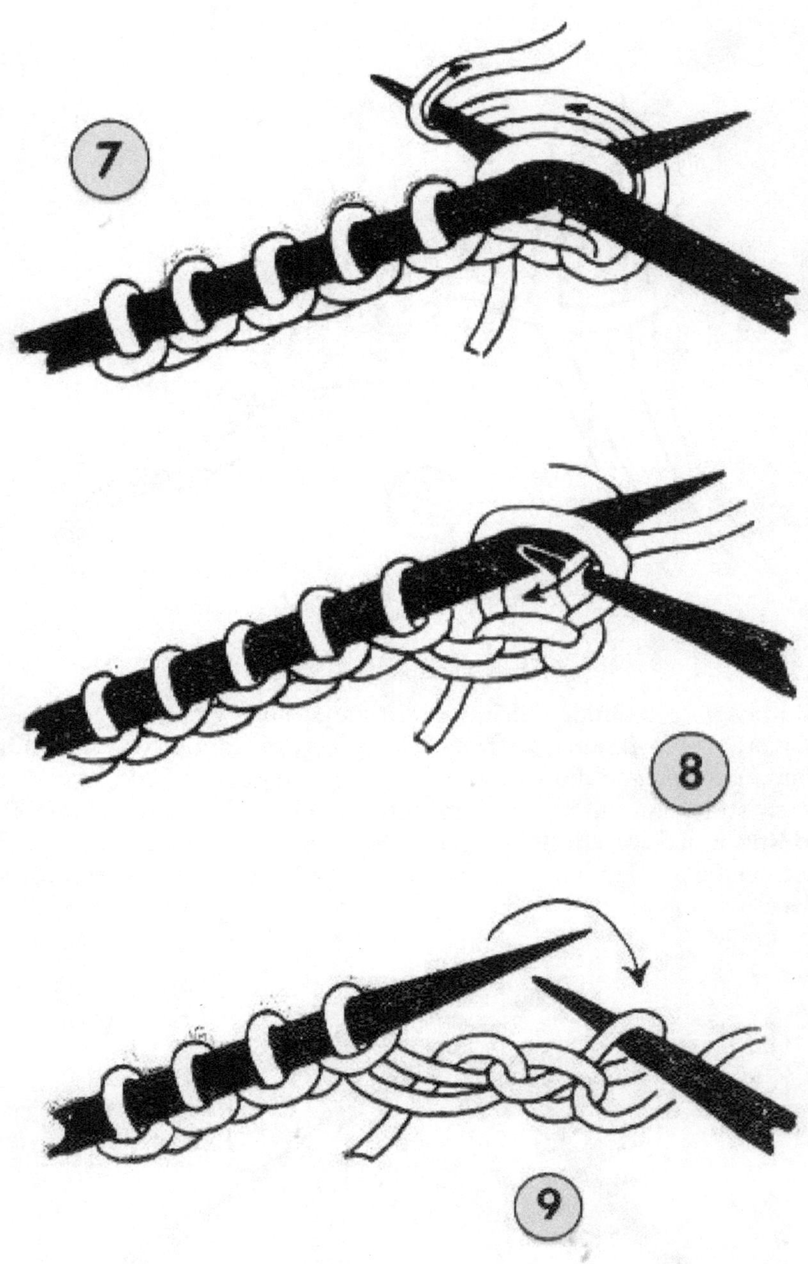

GARTER STITCH

K each st, K each row.

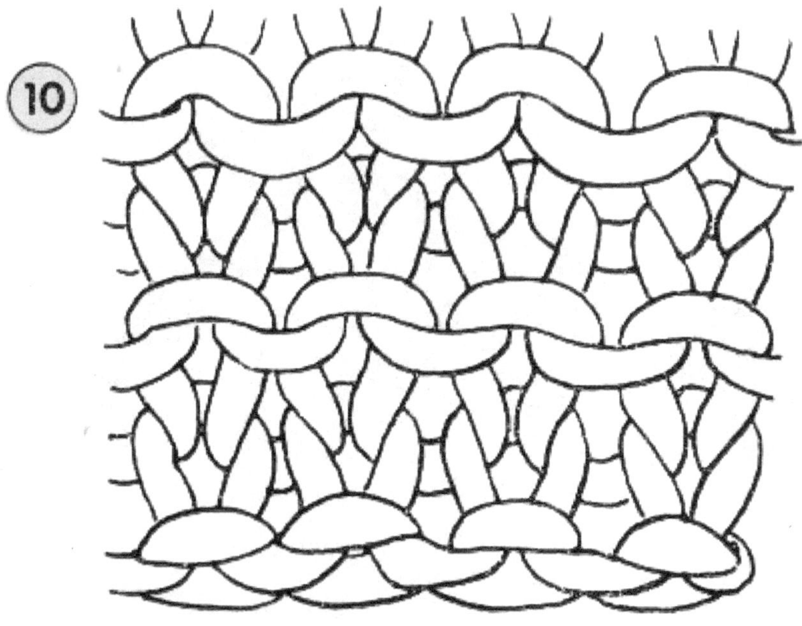

PURLING

Hold work same as for Knitting, but hold yarn to front of work. Follow arrows. * Insert needle from right to left in front of st, yarn around and in back of point of needle, draw through st having new stitch on right needle, slip stitch off left needle. Repeat from * until all stitches are on right needle.

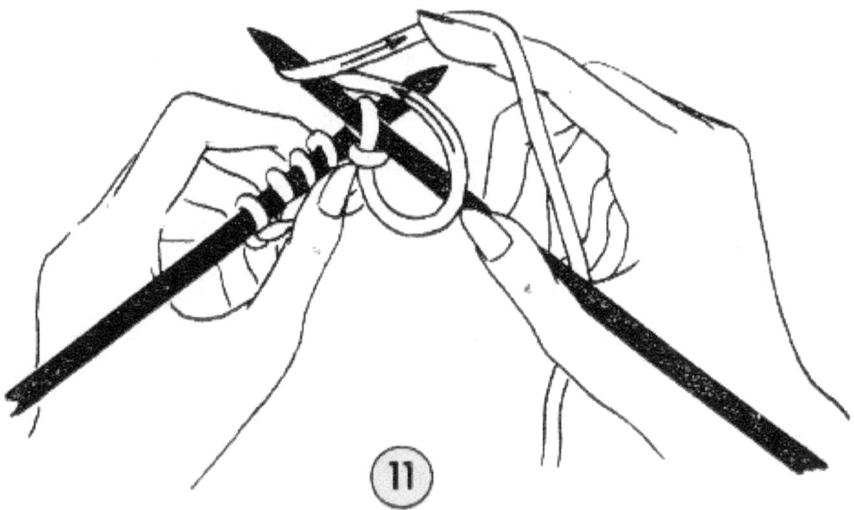

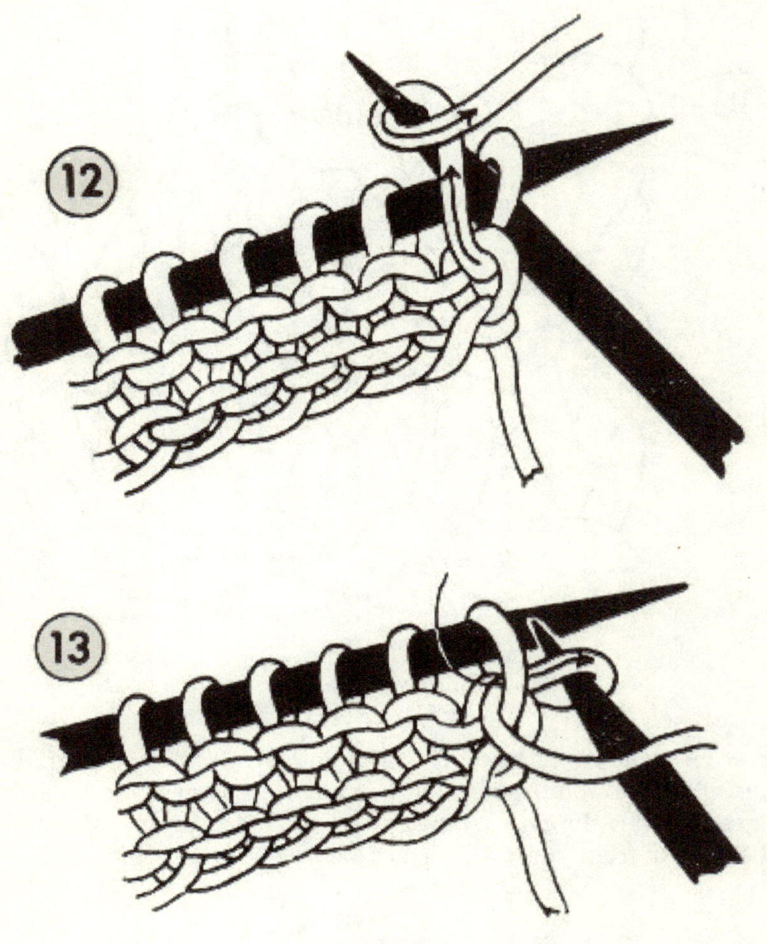

STOCKINETTE STITCH

Knit 1 row, Purl 1 row when working with 2 needles. K each row when working with a circular needle or on 3 or 4 double pointed needles.

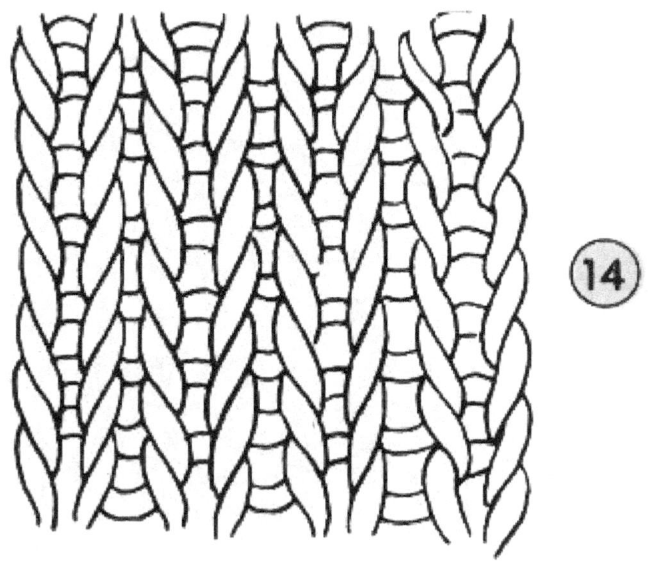

14 KNIT SIDE

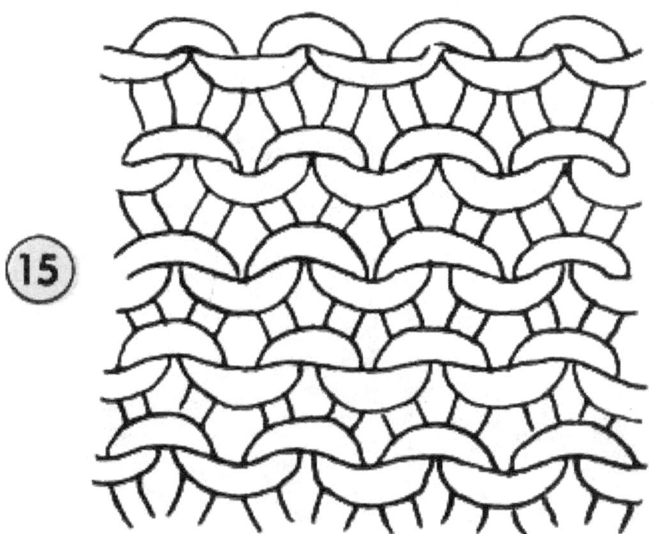

15 PURL SIDE

RIBBING

Ribbing consists of an alternate number of Knit and Purl stitches. In Knit 2, Purl 2 ribbing the number of stitches cast on is usually divisible by 4. **1st ROW**: K

2, P 2 across row. In the next row again start with K 2. In ribbing, the smooth sts are knitted, the sts with rough side are purled. In binding off ribbing Knit the Knit sts and Purl the Purl stitches.

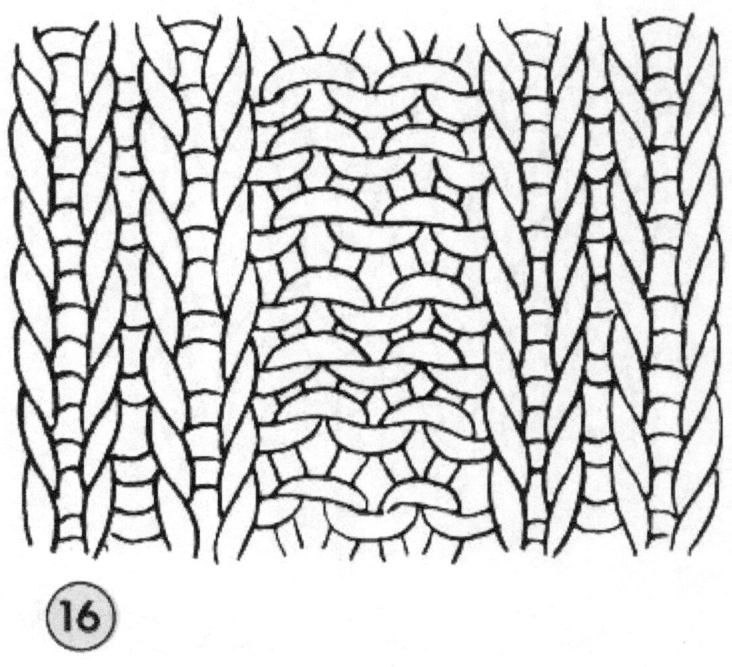

TO DECREASE OR NARROW

In Knitting, Knit 2 sts together (Ill. No. 17), in Purling, Purl 2 sts together.

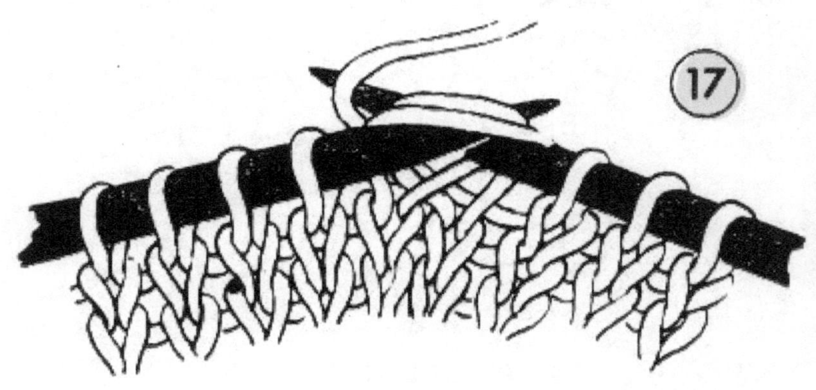

PASS SLIP STITCH OVER (P.S.S.O.)

(another method of decreasing).... In knitting instructions p.s.s.o. means to slip 1 st, K (or P) next st, then pass the slip st over the K (or P) st by inserting left needle into slip st on right needle and passing over the K st on right needle. Follow arrows in illustrations.

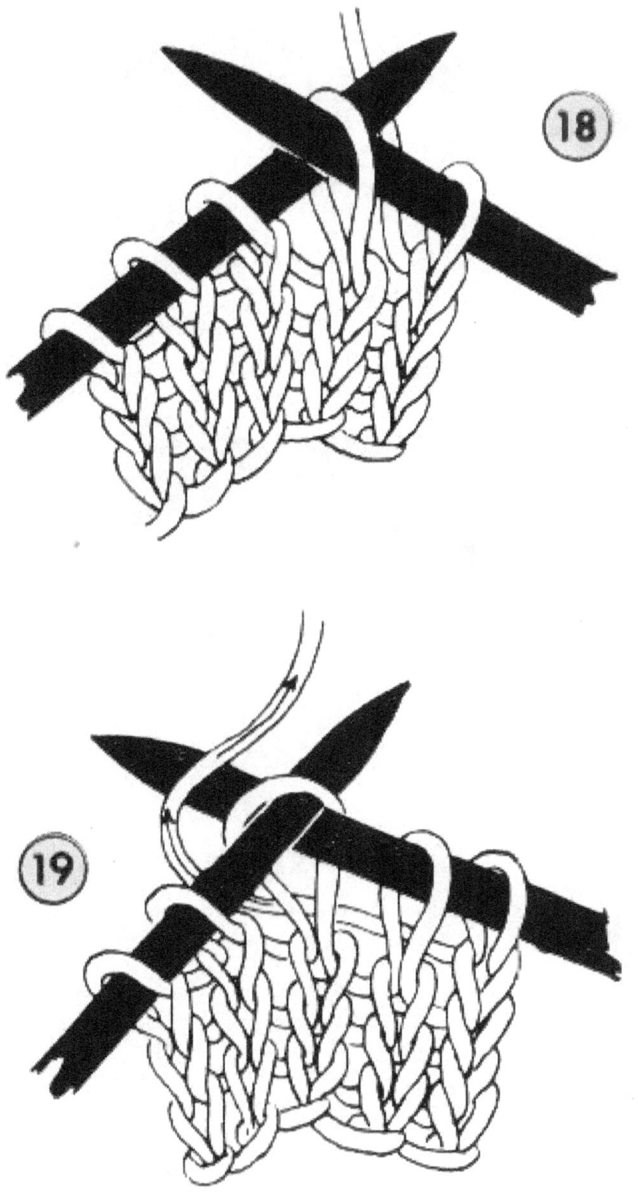

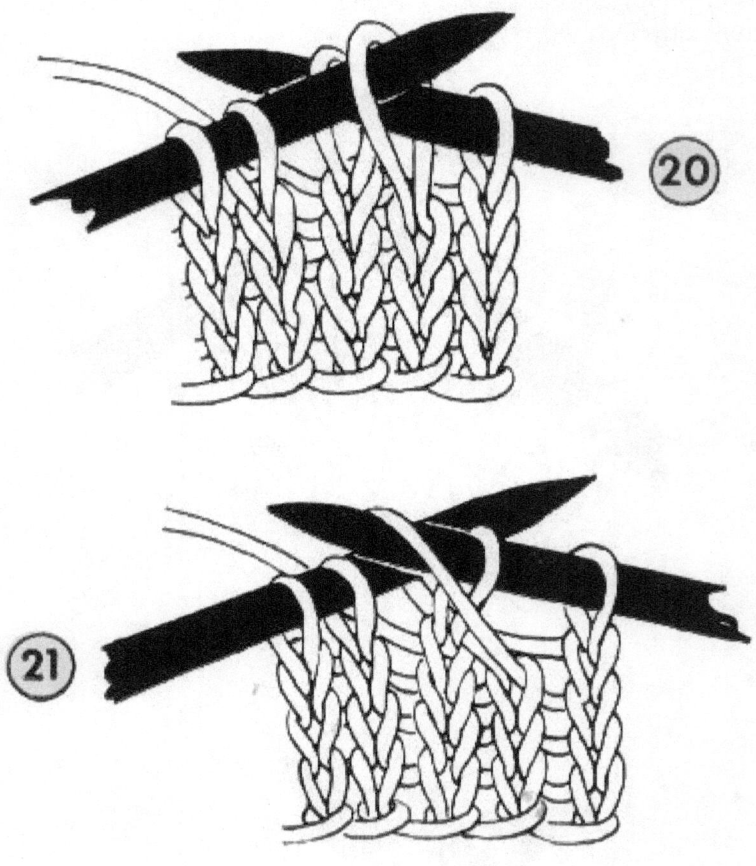

TO INCREASE

Knit or Purl 1 st (as directions call for), but do not slip stitch from left needle (Ill. No. 22 & 23). Knit or Purl into back of same st, then slip stitch off needle (Ill. No. 24).

Illustration shows a Knit increase.

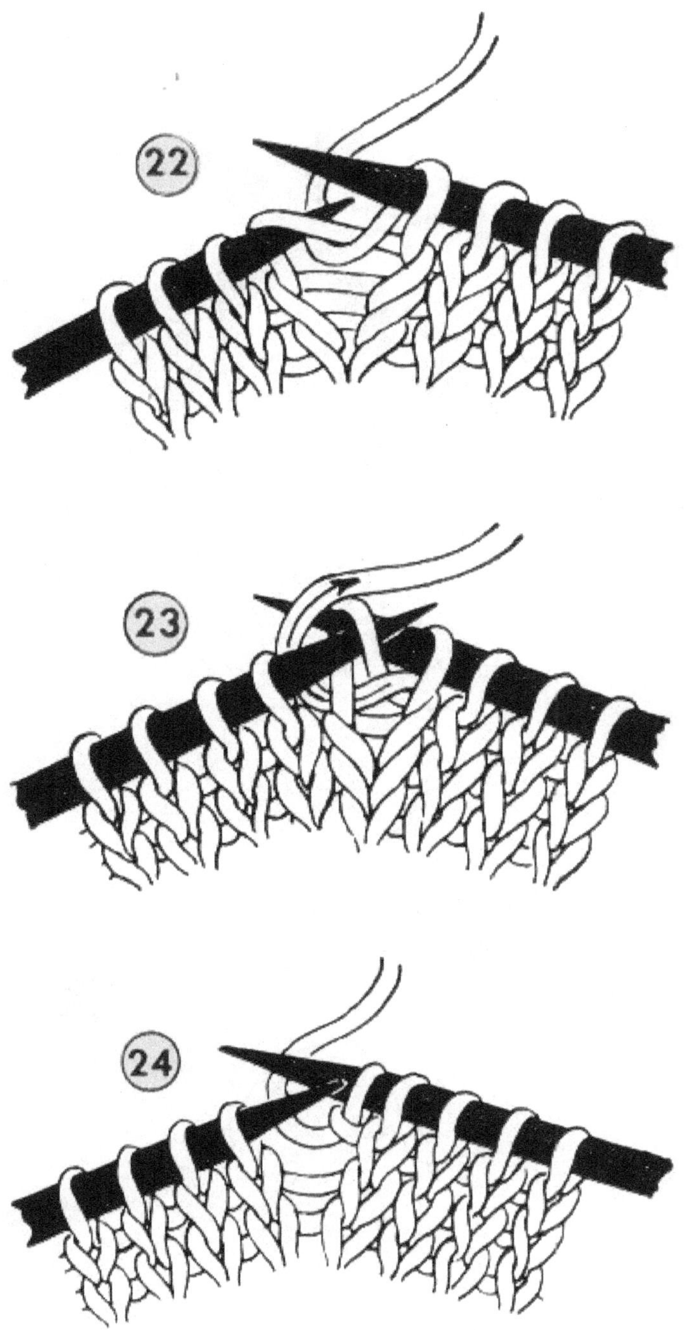

YARN OVER....

Unless otherwise instructed when knitting, bring yarn forward and over right needle to back, K next st. When Purling bring yarn over and under right needle and to front, P next st. The yarn over forms a loop on needle which is worked as a stitch, it is used usually for lacy patterns and beadings.

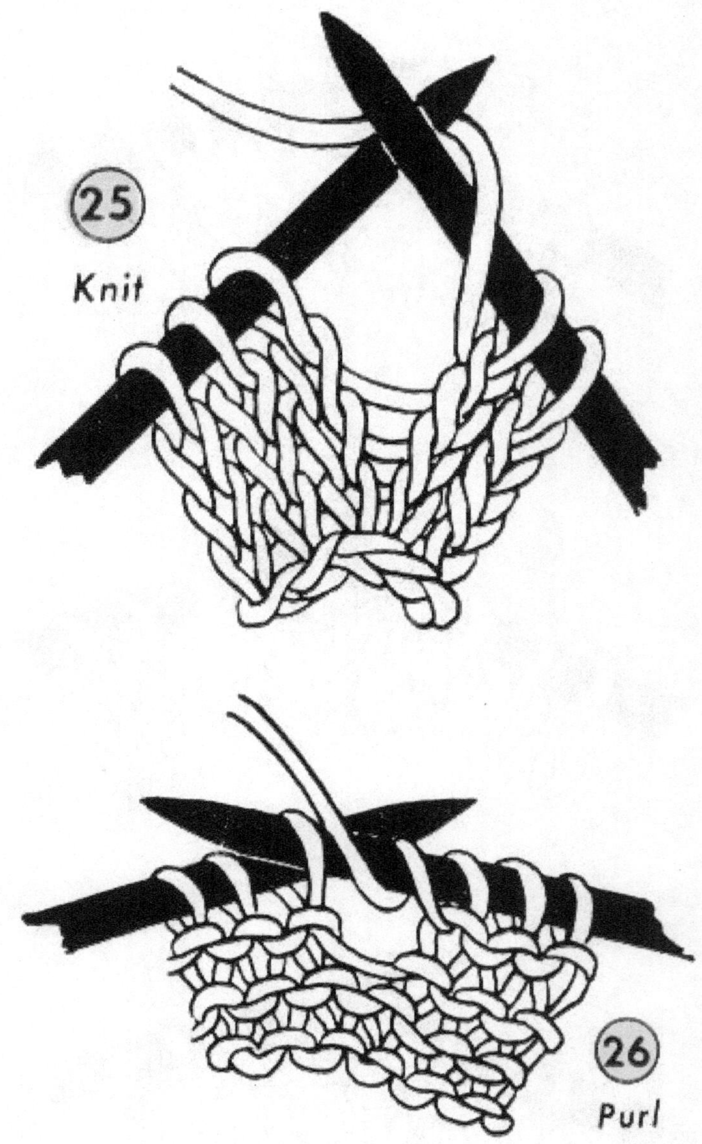

BIND OFF

Do not bind off too tightly.

Knitting: K 2 sts, * pass the 1st stitch over the 2nd stitch: follow arrows (Ill. 27, 28, 29), K next st, repeat from * until one stitch remains on right needle, cut yarn and draw through last st.

PURLING: P 2 sts, * pass 1st stitch over 2nd stitch, P next st, repeat from * until one stitch remains on right needle, cut yarn and draw through last st. Not illustrated.

IN PATTERN: Either Knit or Purl st to be bound off as it would have been worked in corresponding row of pattern, then bind off for knitting or purling whichever pattern calls for. Not illustrated.

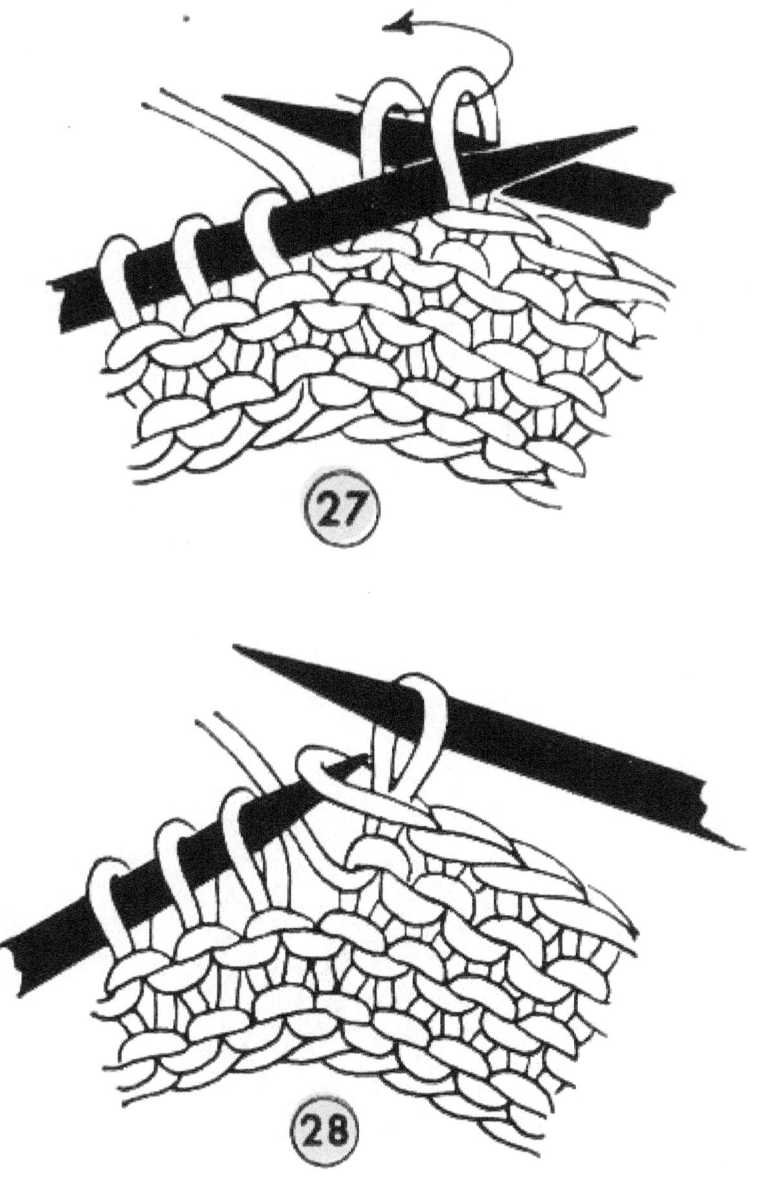

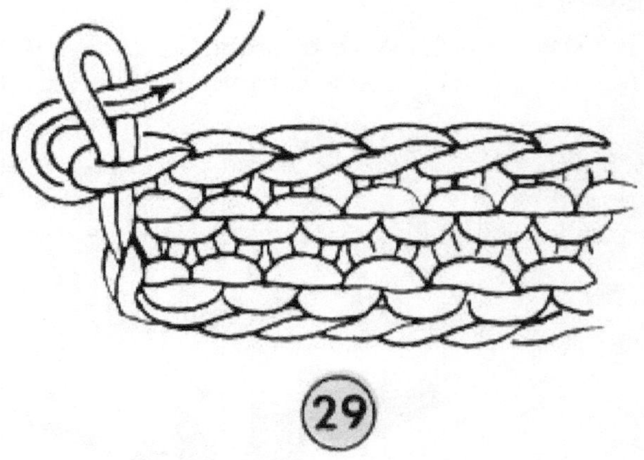

(29)

TO SLIP A STITCH....

Slip one st from left needle to right needle without knitting or purling inserting the right needle in the st as if to Knit unless otherwise directed. When slipping the stitch leave yarn to the wrong side unless directed otherwise.

PICKING UP STITCHES .... DROPPED ST ...

In stockinette stitch pick up stitch on right side of work. Using a crochet hook, insert hook in dropped st, draw yarn to row above through loop forming a new loop. Continue in this manner until you reach the row being worked being careful not to twist the sts. (Ill. No. 30). **PURL** sts are picked up by inserting crochet hook through dropped st from in back of sts. (Ill. No. 31). In **GARTER STITCH** alternate the two movements. **RIPPING BACK**: Unravel work to within the last row of point desired. Rip the last row a stitch at a time placing each stitch on a free needle, preferably a finer double pointed needle, then place these sts back on size needle you are using. Continue knitting as directed.

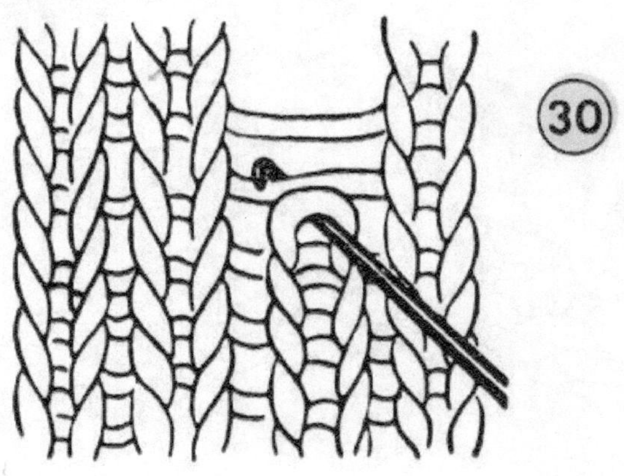

(30)

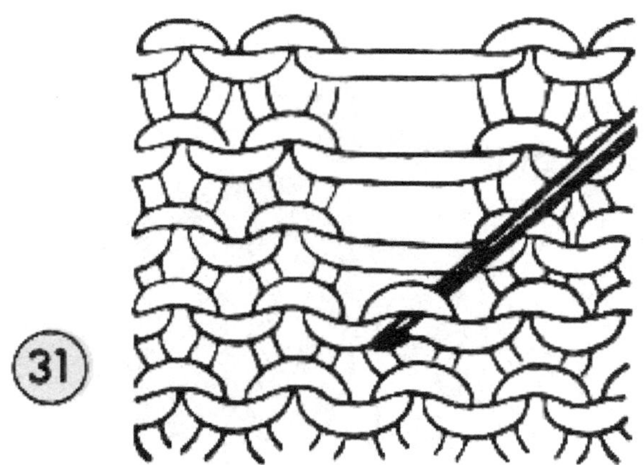

PICKING UP STITCHES ...

around neck and armholes is usually done with smaller needles. Hold the work with right side toward you and work from right to left. Insert right needle into the first st from edge, pick up stitches (Ill. No. 32). When picking up stitches on an irregular edge be sure to pick up a stitch in every row. Always work with the right side toward you unless otherwise directed.

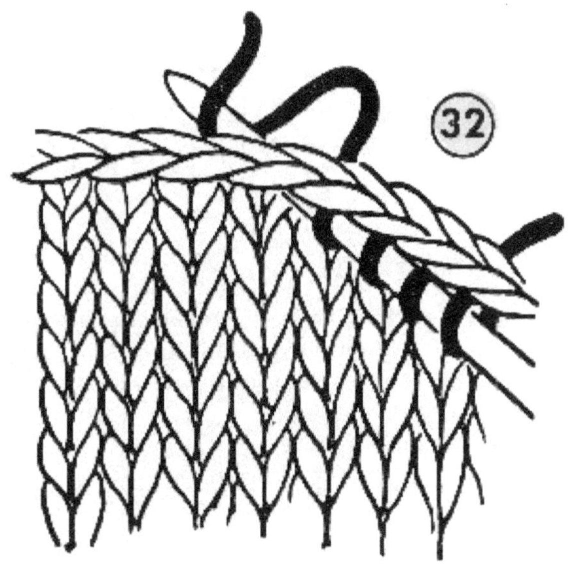

BUTTONHOLES

Work to the point specified. Bind off three or more stitches according to directions and work to end of row. In the following row work to the bound off sts and cast on the same number of stitches bound off in previous row and complete row. (Ill. No. 33 and 34).

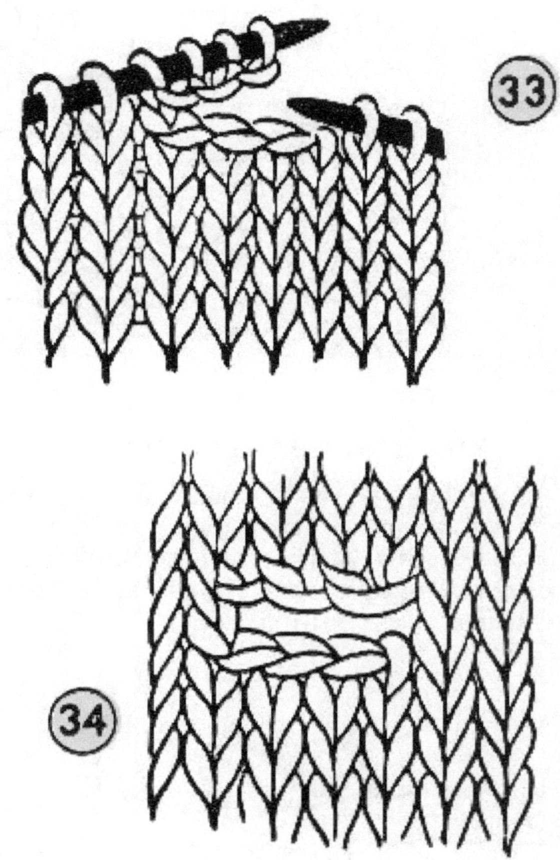

WEAVING TOE

Cut yarn leaving about a 14 inch length, thread this into a darning needle, * insert needle through first st of first needle as if knitting and slip stitch off needle, pass through next stitch as if purling and leave stitch on needle, draw yarn through first st of back needle as if purling and slip stitch off needle, draw yarn through next stitch of back needle as if knitting and leave stitch on needle, repeat from * until all stitches have been worked, fasten neatly.

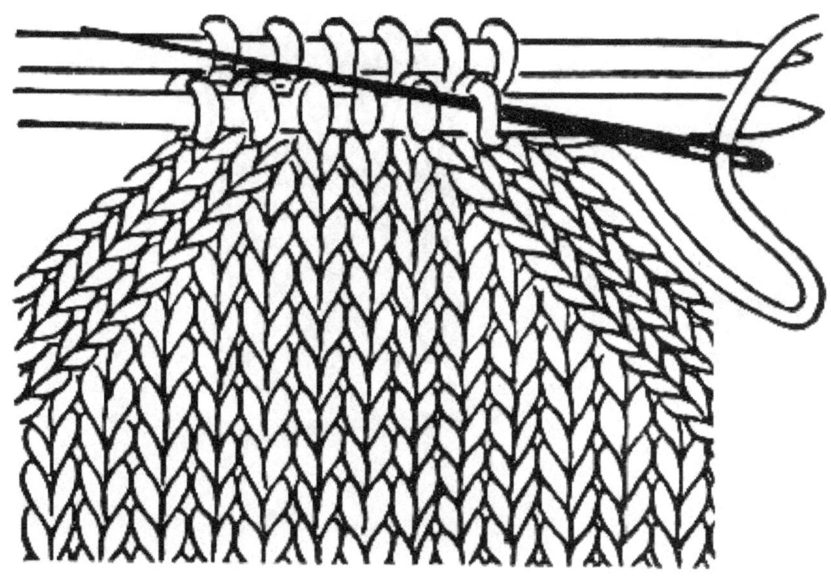

DUPLICATE STITCH

This is the stitch used most often for embroidering a desired motif on a knitted article. It is worked by: * bringing needle through center of stitch from the wrong side to right side of work—see ill. A. Following the outline of the knit stitch above, draw the yarn across the back of the two strands of this stitch—see ill. A and B—return needle to the center of the same stitch—see ill. B—and draw yarn through. Repeat from * starting next stitch by bringing needle through center of stitch to be duplicated—see ill. C.

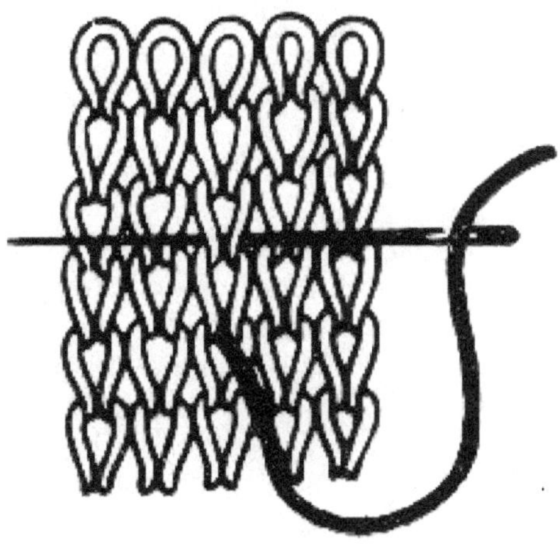

ILL. A

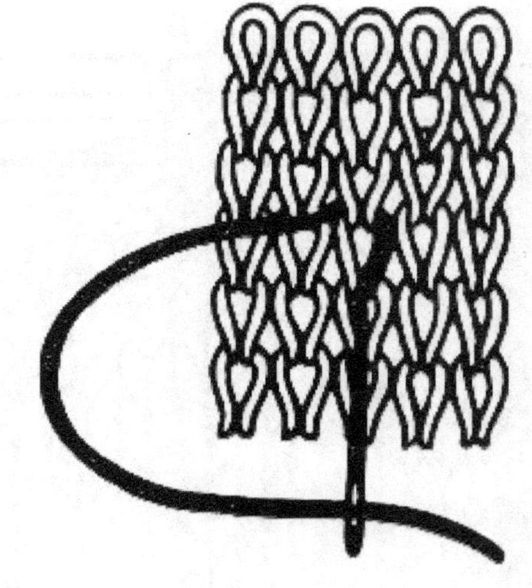

ILL. B

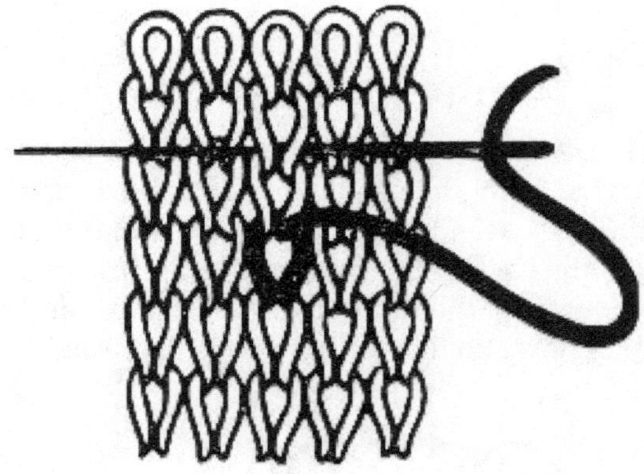

ILL. C

CHANGING COLORS....

At the end of a row, tie in new color and continue in pattern. In Scandinavian, Fair Isle or Ski patterns the additional colors are carried on the wrong side of work. Designs of this type are usually worked from a chart with a color code. When changing colors always twist yarns around each other to prevent a hole. If color is carried over more than 4 sts, the carried color should be twisted around the yarn that is being worked to prevent loose lengths on wrong side. Twist the yarn in following manner; pick up carried color, before knitting st in usual manner twist over yarn that is carried. Cut colors only when you are through with that color leaving about a 4 or 5 inch length to be fastened later with a yarn sewing needle. If designs to be worked are separated or only 1 design is worked in a corner of garment, use bobbins (see page 6) to work design.

GENERAL INFORMATION

Directions are given for Ladies small (size 12, Bust 32). Changes for Ladies' Medium (Size 14, Bust 34) and Large (Size 16, Bust 36) are given in parentheses. Men's small (Size and Chest 38), Medium (Size and Chest 40) and Large (Size and Chest 42) are given in bold face type.

CHANGING SIZES

NOTE: When working with pattern sts ADD or SUBTRACT the multiple of sts or repeats necessary to work one inch of gauge for size desired.

LARGER: (1) For each size larger than given, ADD the number of sts called for in GAUGE to make 1 inch to both back and front cast on sts.

(2) Continue to follow directions given to armhole shaping or desired length to armhole. Bind off 2 sts more for each size larger. Work ¼ inch more in length.

(3) **SHAPE SHOULDERS**: Bind off 2 sts more each shoulder for each size larger.

(4) **SLEEVES**: Add 2 sts more in cuff, then 2 sts more in last row of ribbing. Bind off 2 sts more each side at underarm.

SMALLER: (1) For each size smaller than size given, SUBTRACT the number of sts called for in GAUGE equal to 1 inch from both front and back cast on sts.

(2) Continue to follow directions to armhole shaping or desired length to armhole. Bind off 2 sts less for each size smaller. Work ¼ inch less in length for each size smaller.

(3) **SHAPE SHOULDERS**: Bind off 2 sts less for each size smaller.

(4) **SLEEVES**: Subtract 4 sts at cuff and bind off 2 sts less each side at underarm.

CHILD'S OR IN-BETWEEN SIZE

If child's garment is desired or if you are not a regular size, work as follows:

(1) Take chest or bust measure. Divide the figure in half (half is front, half is back).

(2) Multiply this figure (the half of chest measure) by sts (or rows) necessary to equal gauge.

(3) Follow directions given, working back and front to desired length to underarm. Work armhole shaping in proportion to directions given. Work armhole desired length. Shape shoulder proportionately to directions being followed. Work sleeves in proportion to added or subtracted sts.

(4) Always have same number of rows on back and front of sweater. Work

same amount of rows for both sleeves.

BLOCKING AND FINISHING

Blocking is method used to shape a garment for a "professional look". Steps to follow:

1—Conceal all ends: run ends through several stitches on wrong side. If yarn is heavy or bulky, split strand and run ends through several stitches.

2—Determine whether garment is to be washed. If so, wash each section separately by hand or machine wash garment according to specific instructions on yarn label or commercial laundering product. Most garments stretch larger when wet. Care, therefore, should be taken in handling wet sections. Squeeze gently in the washing, DO NOT TWIST or WRING. Rinse thoroughly. Place in turkish towel and squeeze out excess moisture. Place on turkish towel to dry. If sections of garment appear to be too big, adjust sections to measure by pushing sections into slight puckers. Puckers will disappear when sections dry.

3—Always use the stitch gauge given as a guide for blocking. Instructions are written for the average in any size, see page 14 for our sizes. Any slight adjustment for individual size should be made in the blocking.

4—After measurements have been determined, place the sections individually and wrong side up on a well padded surface or table. It is sometimes helpful to draw outline on brown paper or heavy tissue paper. With rust proof pins, pin each section to measurement spacing pins about ½ inch apart.

5—Place a wet pressing cloth over a section. Using a rotary motion, hold iron as close as possible to section allowing steam to penetrate, but DO NOT at any time let iron rest on garment. Leave sections on pressing table until thoroughly dry.... Do not hurry this process.

6—Always bear in mind that cables and rib patterns have a tendency to pull in or shrink back. Each section should be blocked about 2 inches more than desired measure, but should NEVER be pressed flat. Also some patterns are especially designed for a textured effect. They too should NEVER be pressed flat. Never press ribbing of cuffs, waistband or neckline.

7—After all sections have been blocked garment is now ready for finishing. Seams may be woven (see illustrations for weaving lengthwise and crosswise seams) or back stitched (see illustration page 31), or by sewing machine.

a—**To weave lengthwise seam**: thread tapestry needle with a single strand of matching yarn. Hold lengthwise edges together, right sides up. Insert needle in center of st on right side, pass under two rows and pull yarn through to right side. Insert needle in corresponding row of left side, draw yarn through in same way. Work from side to side in this manner taking care to keep seam elastic, matching rows, patterns, stripes, etc. **To weave a crosswise seam**: hold crosswise edges together. Starting at right edge, insert needle under two loops of stitch on top section, insert needle down through center of next stitch and up through center of next stitch on lower section. Continue in same manner working alternately into top section and then into lower section until seam is completed taking care to keep seam elastic and matching patterns, etc.

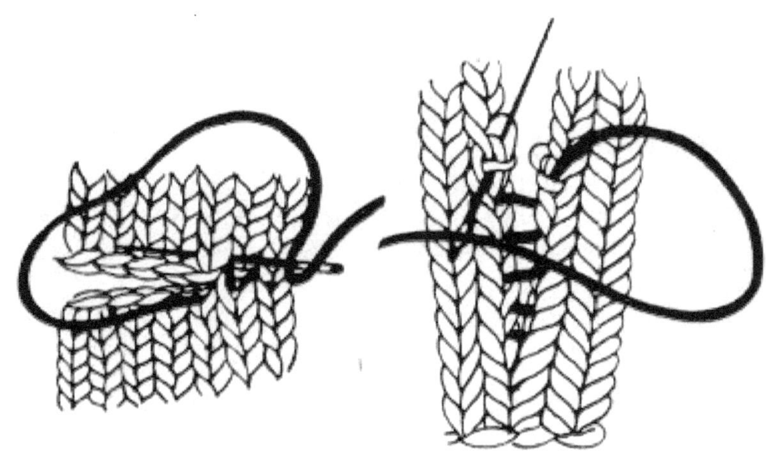

b—**Back stitching**: place right sides of sections to be seamed together. Pin, keeping edges even and matching rows or patterns. With tapestry needle and matching yarn back stitch close to edge taking care not to draw stitches too tight and keeping seam elastic.

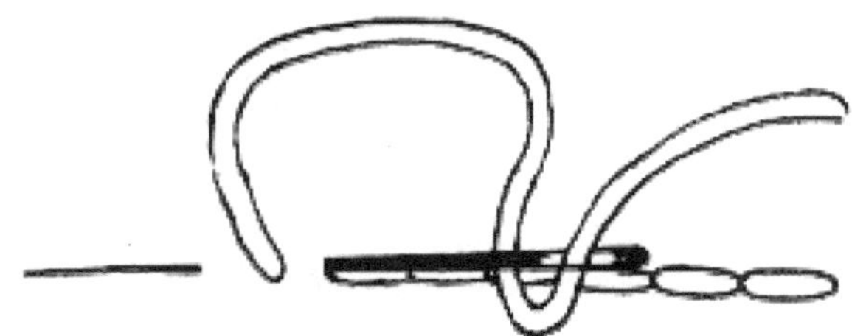

c—**Sewing machine**: loosen tension on machine as you would for jersey or any stretchy fabric. Place right sides together and pin. Baste seam being careful not to draw stitches too tight. Remove pins. With matching thread machine stitch seam. If yarn is bulky or fuzzy sew over tissue paper. Remove paper when finished.

8—After garment is all assembled, carefully steam seams flat and even.

TO SHORTEN ...

(No hem desired). Determine length you desire; place a marker. Cut through one st at side seam about 2 rows below marker. * Pick up cut end and draw through several sts, cut this length close as possible to work. This drawn length will tighten sts. After length has been cut straighten edge taking care with loose sts. Place loose sts on free needle. Repeat from * until row has been ripped and sts have been placed on needle. With free needle bind off—or—attach yarn on P side, and with crochet hook work a slip stitch (see page 30) in each st, turn. Work a slip stitch in each st, cut yarn. If a hem is desired, allow for hem and complete same as above. Turn hem to wrong side and tack in place.

TO LENGTHEN ...

(If a sufficient amount of same dye lot is available). Cut off cast on edge in same manner as above. Pick up loose sts and knit to length desired. If there is a ribbing on section to be lengthened, cut into the row above the ribbing, then add to length. If you do not have enough of same dye lot to work garment to length desired, we suggest working a stripe of contrasting color and finishing with same color as garment.

SNUG AND COMFORTABLE ... AND EASY TO MAKE

KNITTED AFGHAN SIZE: 48 × 60 INCHES

Materials Required:

AMERICAN THREAD COMPANY "DAWN" KNITTING WORSTED 3-4 ounce skeins each Lime, Putty, Cinnamon, Potter Gold and Antique Gold.

1 Pr. Knitting Needles No. 8 OR ANY SIZE NEEDLES WHICH WILL RESULT IN STITCH GAUGE BELOW.

Plastic Crochet Hook Size H

GAUGE: 4 sts = 1 inch. Each block is a 12 inch square Approximate size: 48 × 60 inches.

SEED ST BLOCK: With Lime cast on 48 sts. **1st ROW:** * K 1, P 1, repeat from * across row. **2nd ROW:** * P 1, K 1, repeat from * across row. Repeat last 2 rows for seed st pattern. Work even in pattern until block measures 12 inches from beg. Bind off. Work 1 more block in same manner. Then work 2 blocks in each remaining color in same manner (10 blocks).

DOUBLE SEED ST BLOCK: With Lime cast on 48 sts. **1st and 2nd ROWS:** * K 2, P 2, repeat from * across row. **3rd and 4th ROWS:** * P 2, K 2, repeat from * across row. Repeat these 4 rows for double seed st pattern. Work even until block measures 12 inches from beg. Bind off. Work 1 more block in same manner. Then work 2 blocks in each remaining color in same manner.

FINISHING: With matching color work a row of s c all around each block working 3 s c in each corner, 1 s c in each st across lower and top edges (46 s c), 1 s c in every other row across sides (39 s c) (S c: insert hook in st, pull yarn through, y o hook and pull through 2 loops). Weave 5 × 4 blocks tog through loop in back of each s c having the seed st blocks in the 1st and 3rd rows and the double seed st blocks in the 2nd and 4th rows arranging colors as follows: **1st ROW:** Putty, Cinnamon, Antique Gold, Potter Gold and Lime. **2nd ROW:** Lime, Potter Gold, Putty, Antique Gold and Cinnamon. **3rd ROW:** Potter Gold, Antique Gold, Lime, Cinnamon and Putty. **4th ROW:** Cinnamon, Putty, Potter Gold, Lime and Antique Gold.

FRINGE: Wind all colors over a 3 inch cardboard, cut one end. Matching colors to blocks, take 2 strands, double in half and with crochet hook loop through every other st all around afghan.

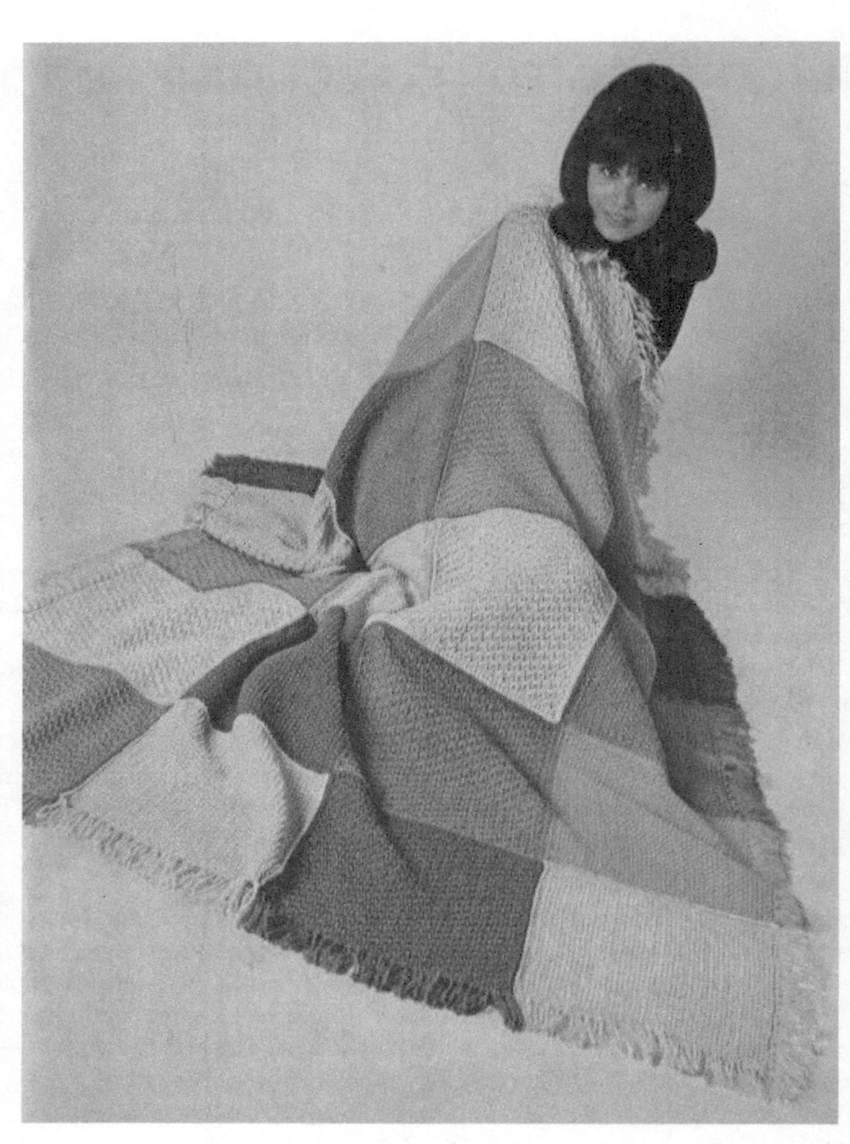

FIVE FANCY STITCHES—LOOK HARD TO DO—BUT EASY TO MAKE

PATTERN NO. 1

Cast on 35 sts. **1st ROW**: K across row. **2nd ROW**: K 1, * yarn in back of work, sl 1 as if to P, K 1, repeat from * across row. **3rd ROW**: K 1, * yarn to front, sl 1 as if to P, K 1, repeat from * across row. **4th ROW**: K across row. Repeat these 4 rows for pattern.

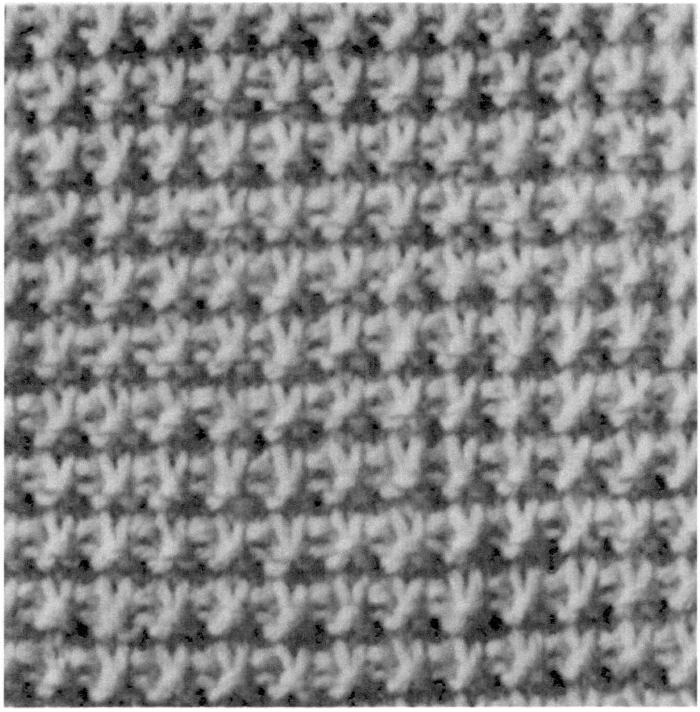

PATTERN NO. 2

Cast on 34 sts. **1st ROW**: K 2, * Y O, sl 1, K 2 tog, p.s.s.o., Y O, K 3, repeat from * across row ending with K last 2 sts. **2nd ROW**: P across row. **3rd ROW**: K 5, * Y O, sl 1, K 2 tog, p.s.s.o., Y O, K 3, repeat from * across row ending with Y O, K 2. **4th ROW**: P across row. Repeat these 4 rows for pattern.

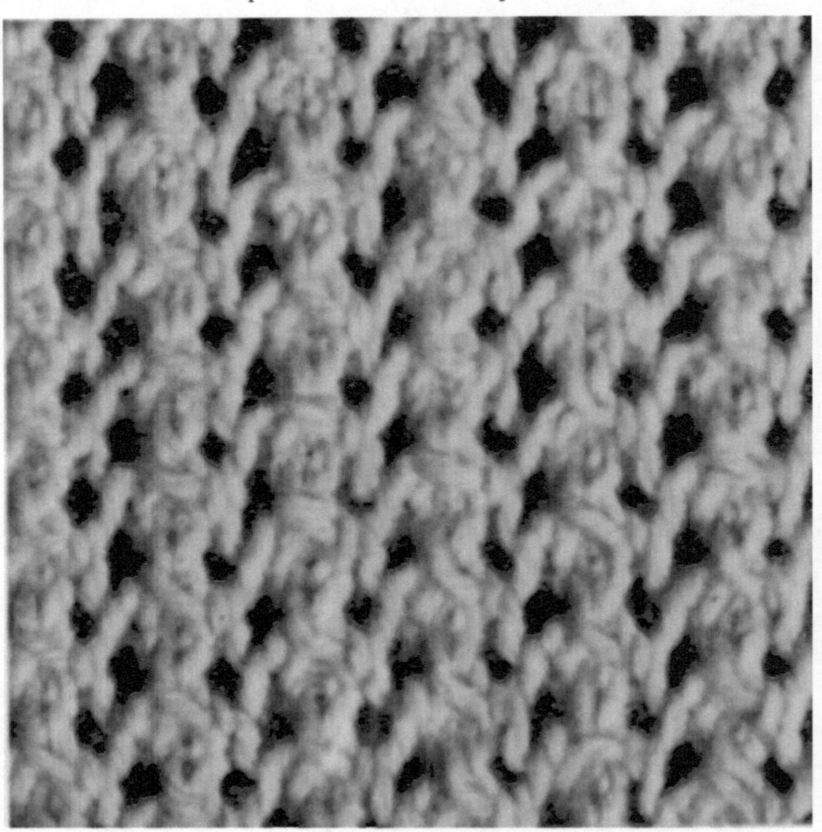

PATTERN NO. 3

Cast on 36 sts. **1st ROW**: * K 2, P 2, repeat from * across row. Repeat 1st row 7 times. **9th, 10th, 11th and 12th ROWS**: K across each row. Repeat these 12 rows for pattern.

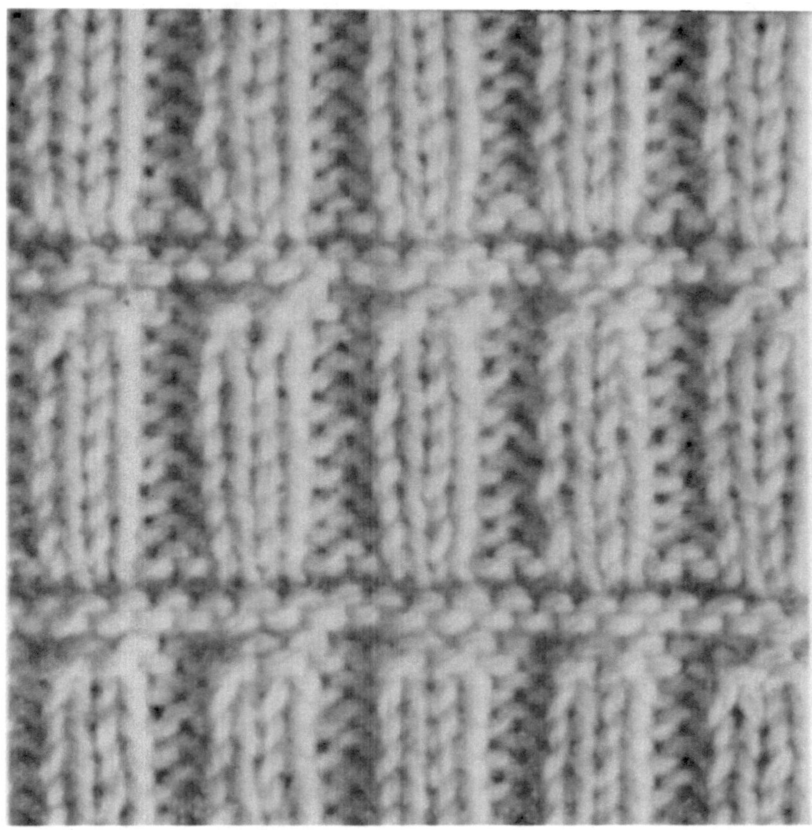

PATTERN NO. 4

Cast on 35 sts. **1st ROW**: K 3, P 3, K 6, P 3, K 5, P 3, K 6, P 3, K 3. **2nd ROW**: P 3, K 3, P 6, K 3, P 5, K 3, P 6, K 3, P 3. Repeat last 2 rows 3 times. **9th ROW**: K 3, P 3, sl next 3 sts on d p n and hold in front of work, K next 3 sts, K 3 sts from d p n (cable twist), P 3, K 5, P 3, cable twist, P 3, K 3. **10th ROW**: Repeat 2nd row. **NEXT 8 ROWS**: Repeat 1st and 2nd rows 4 times. Repeat from 9th row for pattern.

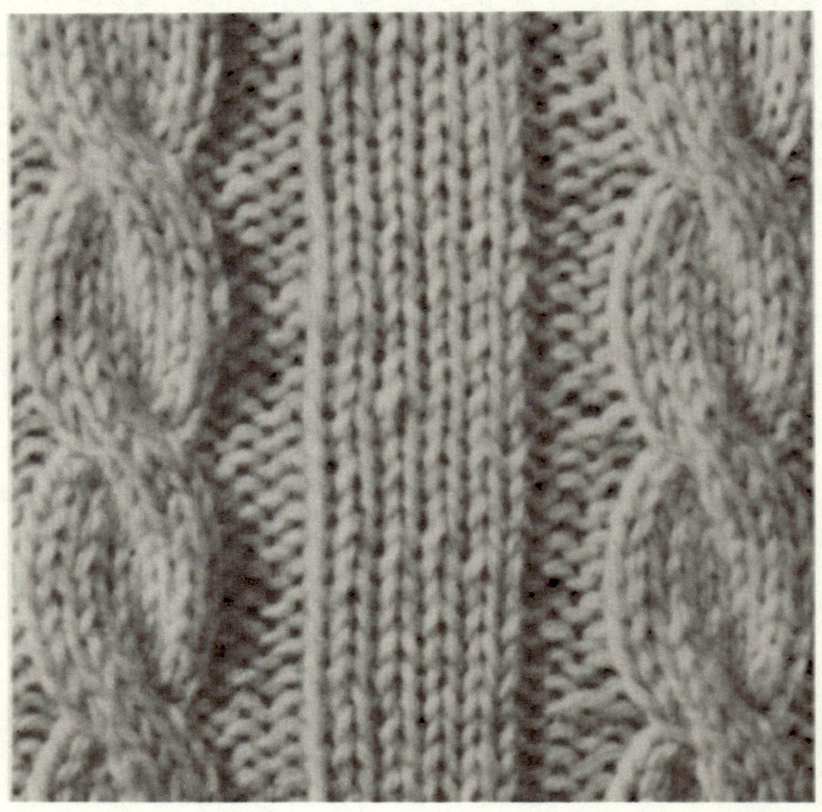

PATTERN NO. 5

Cast on 36 sts. **1st and 3rd ROWS**: K 4, * P 4, K 4, repeat from * 3 times. **2nd and 4th ROWS**: P 4, * K 4, P 4, repeat from * 3 times. **5th and 7th ROWS**: P 4, * K 4, P 4, repeat from * 3 times. **6th and 8th ROWS**: K 4, * P 4, K 4, repeat from * 3 times. Repeat these 8 rows 7 times.

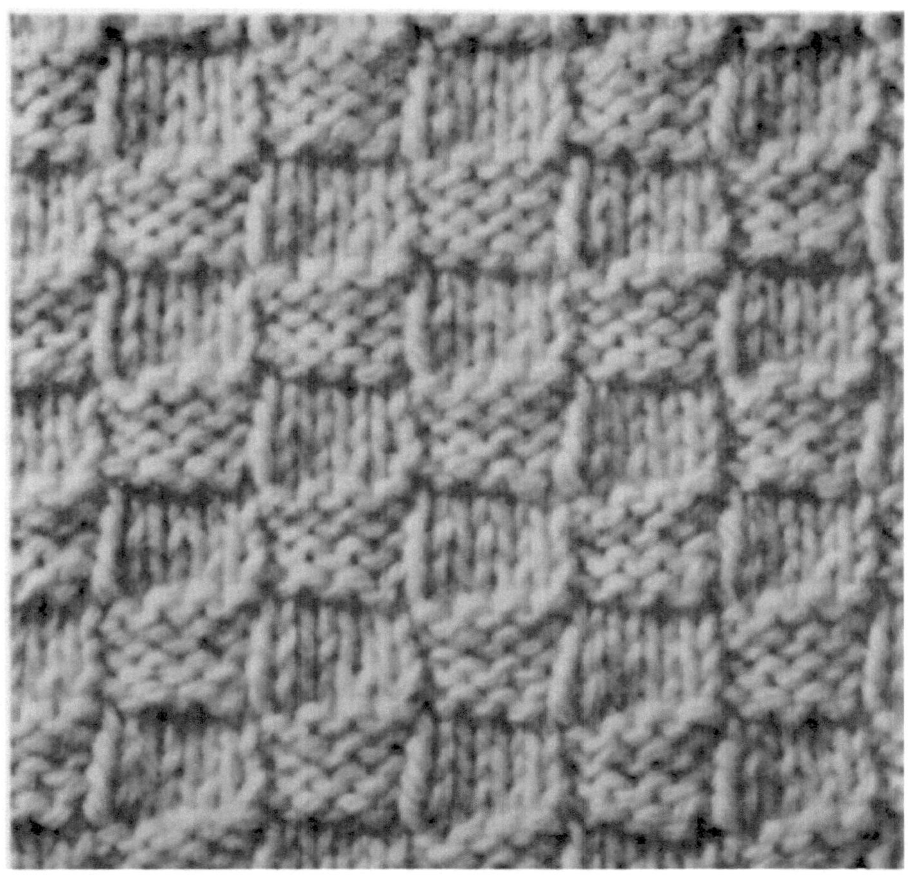

PLAIN SOCKS FOR A GO-GO GUY

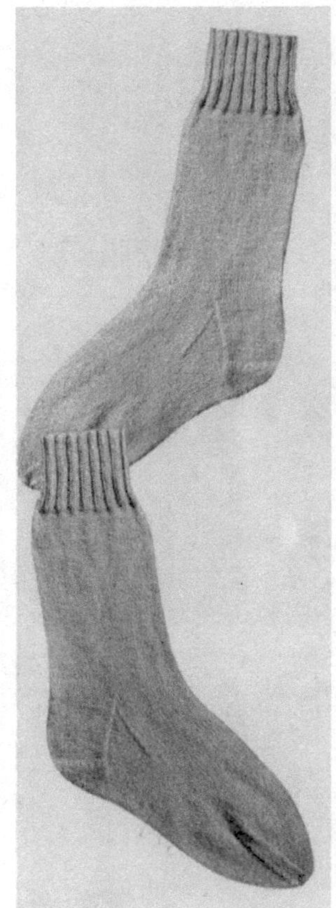

Materials Required:

AMERICAN THREAD COMPANY "DAWN" NYLON or "DAWN" DE LUXE FINGERING YARN

3 ounces Sand

1 Set Double Pointed Knitting Needles No. 1 OR ANY SIZE NEEDLES WHICH WILL RESULT IN STITCH GAUGE BELOW.

GAUGE: 8 sts = 1 inch.

NOTE: For reinforcing toes (and heels) combine 1 strand of **"Dawn"** Nylon Reinforcing Yarn, Article N-7 with yarn and knit per instructions.

Cast on 72 sts, divide sts on 3 needles (24 sts on each needle), join. Place a marker at beginning of round. Work in ribbing of K 2, P 2 for 2½ inches. Change to stockinette st (K each round), work even until sock measures 8 inches from beg. **HEEL**: At beg of round divide sts as follows: K and sl next 18 sts on a needle, K and sl next 18 sts on another needle. Working on remaining sts only K 1 row, P 1 row for 2½ inches ending with a P row. **START TO TURN HEEL: 1st ROW**: K 20, sl 1, K 1, pass sl st over K st (p.s.s.o.), K 1, turn. **2nd ROW**: Sl 1, P 5, P 2 tog, P 1, turn. **3rd ROW**: Sl 1, K 6, sl 1, K 1, p.s.s.o., K 1, turn. **4th ROW**: Sl 1, P 7, P 2 tog, P 1, turn. Continue in the above manner until all sts have been worked ending with a P row. Divide these sts on 2 needles. K 10 sts on needle, pick up and K 17 sts on right side of heel (1st needle), work across 36 sts of instep (2nd needle), pick up and K 17 sts on left side of heel, K remaining sts of heel to this needle (3rd needle). **NEXT ROUND**: Work even, then dec **every other round** as follows: 1st needle: K to within 3 sts of end of needle, K 2 tog, K 1; 2nd needle: K across, 3rd needle: K 1, sl 1, K 1, p.s.s.o., K to end of round. Dec in same manner until there are 72 sts on needles. Work even until foot measures 7½ inches or 2 inches less than desired length from center back of heel. **Decrease for Toe**: 1st needle: K to within 3 sts of end of needle, K 2 tog, K 1; 2nd needle: K 1, sl 1, K 1, p.s.s.o., work to within 3 sts of end of same needle, K 2 tog, K 1; 3rd needle: K 1, sl 1, K 1, p.s.s.o., work to end of round. K 1 round even. Repeat these 2 rounds until 16 sts remain (8 sts on instep needle and 4 sts on each back needle). Sl sts of back needles to one needle. Weave sts together following directions on page 13.

MEN'S SHORT SOCKS

Follow directions for plain socks working only 2 inches of ribbing and 4 inches of stockinette st before starting heel.

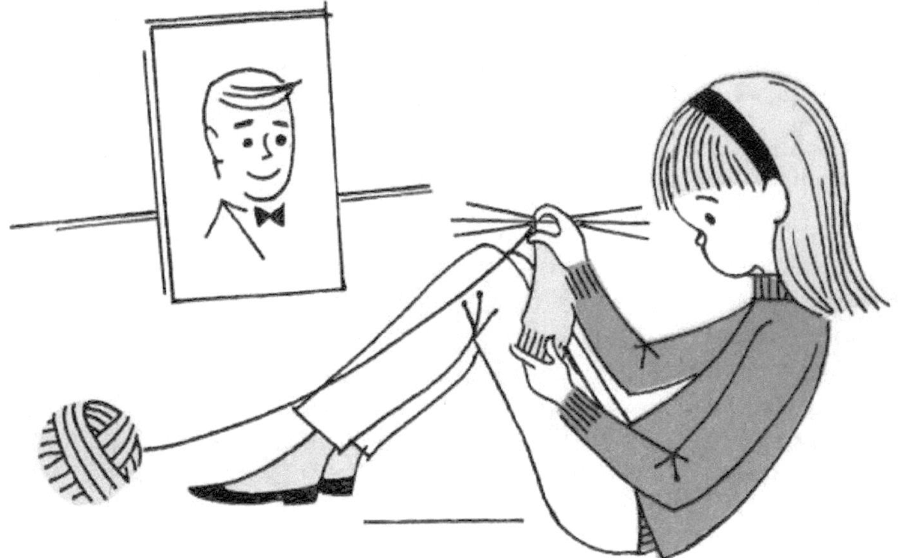

DOLLS AND GUYS TWO NEEDLE MITTENS

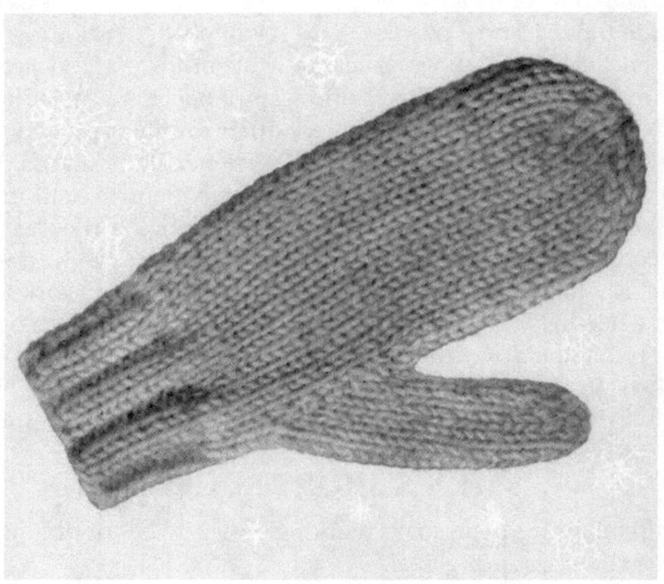

Materials Required:

AMERICAN THREAD COMPANY "DAWN" KNITTING WORSTED 2 Ounces Ladies Small, 3 Ounces (all remaining sizes) Canary.

1 Pr. Knitting Needles No. 5 and No. 7 OR ANY SIZE NEEDLES WHICH WILL RESULT IN STITCH GAUGE BELOW:

GAUGE for No. 7 Needles: 5 sts = 1 inch; 7 rows = 1 inch.

Directions are given for ladies small size. Changes for medium and large sizes are given in parentheses. Men's sizes given in **bold face** type.

LEFT MITTEN: With No. 5 needles cast on 28 (32, 36) **32 (36, 40)** sts and work in ribbing of K 2, P 2 for 1¾, **2** inches increasing 2 sts for men's small size only in last row of ribbing. Change to No. 7 needles and work in stockinette st (K 1 row, P 1 row) for 6 (6, 8) **8 (8, 10)** rows. **NEXT ROW**: Start Gussett. K 13 (15, 17) **16 (17, 19)** sts, inc 1 st in each of the next 2 sts, K next 13 (15,17) **16 (17, 19)** sts. **NEXT ROW**: P across row. **NEXT ROW**: K 13 (15, 17) **16 (17, 19)** sts, inc in next st, K 2, inc in next st, K to end of row. Continue in stockinette st increasing at Gusset every other row until there are 40 (44, 50) **46 (50, 54)** sts on needle ending with a K row. **NEXT ROW**: P 14 (16, 18) **16 (18, 19)** sts and place on st holder, work next 12 (12, 14) **14**

(**14**, **16**) sts for thumb, place remaining sts on 2nd st holder.

THUMB: Work in stockinette st until thumb measures ¼ inch less than desired length ending with a P row. **NEXT ROW**: K 2 tog, K 2, repeat from across row ending with K-O (K O, K 2 tog) **K 2 tog (K 2 tog, K-O)**. **NEXT ROW**: P across row. **NEXT ROW**: * K 2 tog, K 1, repeat from * across row ending with K-O (K O, K 2) **K 2 (K 2, K-O)**. Cut yarn and draw sts tog. Fasten firmly. Pick up and P sts from 2nd st holder. **NEXT ROW**: K across all sts including sts sts from 1st st holder. There are 28 (32, 36) **32 (36, 38)** sts on needle. Work in stockinette st until mitten measures 1 inch less than desired length ending with a P row. **NEXT ROW**: * K 2 tog, K 3, repeat from * across row ending with K 1 (K 2 tog, K 4) **K 2 tog (K 4, K 1)**. **NEXT ROW**: P across row. **NEXT ROW**: * K 2 tog, K 2, repeat from * across row ending with K 2 tog (K 3, K 3) **K 3 (K 3, K 2 tog)**. **NEXT ROW**: P across row. **NEXT ROW**: * K 2 tog, K 1, repeat from * across row ending with K 2 (all sizes). Cut yarn leaving an 18 inch length. Thread yarn into needle and draw sts tog. Fasten firmly. Sew thumb and side seam.

RIGHT MITTEN: Work same as left mitten.

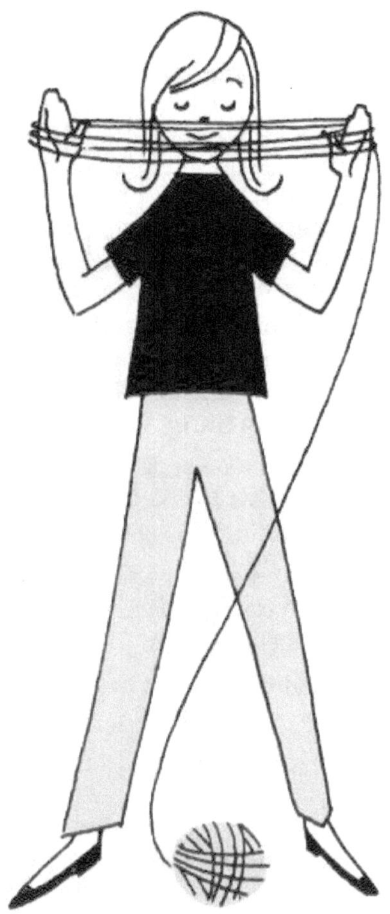

FOR THE YEARLING ... THE SWEATER

SIZE: 6 MONTHS TO 1 YEAR

Materials Required:

AMERICAN THREAD COMPANY "DAWN" ORLON or "DAWN" MEDIUM WEIGHT POMPADOUR

5—1 ounce skeins Baby Pink

1 Pr. Knitting Needles No. 4 OR ANY SIZE NEEDLES WHICH WILL RESULT IN STITCH GAUGE BELOW.

2 Yds. ¼ inch Ribbon for booties and mittens

3¼ yards ¾ inch Ribbon for hat and sweater

GAUGE: 7 sts = 1 inch

SWEATER

Working Back and Fronts at one time cast on 155 sts. **1st ROW**: K 1, * P 1, K 1, repeat from * across. **2nd ROW**: K 1, * P 1, K 1, repeat from * across (seed st). Repeat last 2 rows 3 times. **9th ROW**: K 1, P 1 across 6 sts, K to within 6 sts, P 1, K 1 across last 6 sts (the 6 sts are front borders). **10th ROW**: K 1, P 1 across 6 sts, P to within 6 sts, P 1, K 1 across last 6 sts. Repeat last 2 rows 3 times. Repeat from 1st row twice. **NEXT 8 ROWS**: Work in seed st. **NEXT 2 ROWS**: Repeat 9th and 10th rows. **DIVIDE for FRONTS and BACK in next row.**

RIGHT FRONT: Work 6 sts in seed st, K 33, place these sts on st holder, bind off 3 sts for Armhole, K across 74 sts for BACK (this includes 1 st left on needle from armhole bind off), place remaining 39 sts on stitch holder for **LEFT FRONT**.

BACK: Working in seed st and stockinette stripe pattern as established bind off 3 sts at beg of next row; then dec 1 st each side every other row twice. Work even until armholes measure 4 inches.

SHAPE SHOULDERS: Bind off 11 sts at beg of next 4 rows; bind off remaining sts.

LEFT FRONT: Sl sts from st holder; bind off 3 sts at armhole. Continue in stripes as established dec 1 st at armhole edge every other row twice. Work even until armhole measures 3 inches ending at front edge. **SHAPE NECK**: Bind off 10 sts at beg of next row; then dec 1 st at neck edge every other row twice. Work even until armhole measures same as back armhole. **SHAPE SHOULDER**: Work same as back shoulder.

RIGHT FRONT: Sl sts from st holder onto needle and complete to correspond to left front reversing shaping.

SLEEVES: Cast on 41 sts. Work 8 rows in seed st. Working remainder of sleeve in stockinette st (K 1 row, P 1 row) inc 1 st at beg and end of next row. Then inc 1 st each side every inch 5 times. Work even until sleeve measures 6¾ inches.

SHAPE CAP: Bind off 3 sts at beg of next 2 rows; then bind off 2 sts at beg of every row until 31 sts remain. Bind off remaining sts.

FINISHING: Sew shoulder and sleeve seams. Sew sleeves in position.

NECK EDGE: With right side facing, starting at right front pick up 69 sts all around neck. Work in seed st for ¾ inch; then in K 1, P 1 ribbing for ¾ inch. Bind off in ribbing. Turn ribbing to inside and tack in place. Finish with ribbon ties and rosettes as illustrated.

... AND EASY TO MAKE HAT BOOTIES AND MITTENS

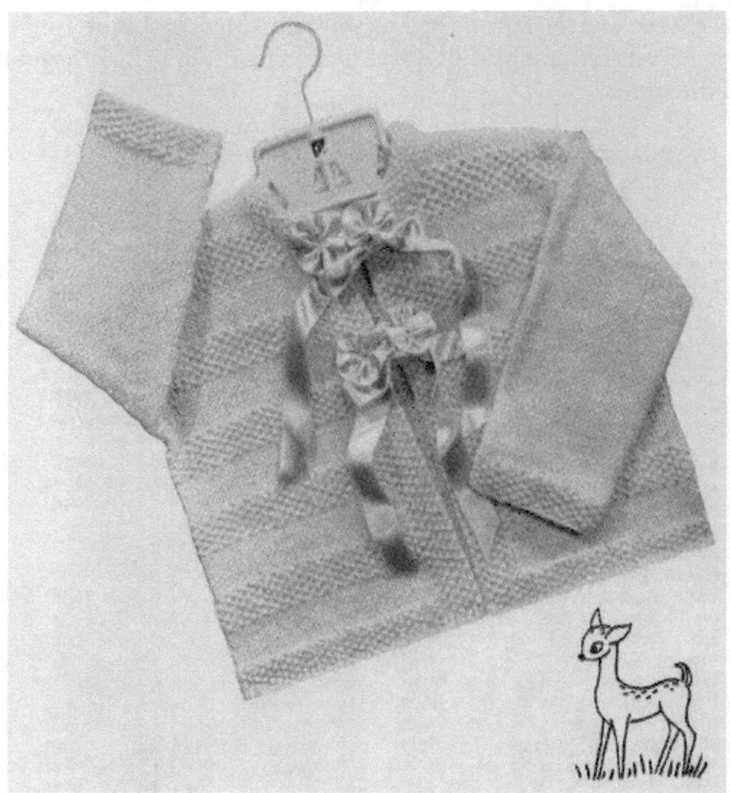

BABY SET

BOOTIES

Cast on 37 sts. Work in seed st for 8 rows. Starting with a P row, work 9 rows in stockinette st. **NEXT ROW:** Work beading; K 1, * Y O, K 2 tog, repeat from * across row. **NEXT ROW:** P. **NEXT ROW:** K 24, sl remaining 13 sts to st holder, turn, P 11, sl remaining 13 sts to st holder. Work back and forth in stockinette st for 2 inches on 11 sts for instep, ending with a K row. Pick up 10 sts on side of instep, K across 13 sts from st holder; turn, P across all sts picking up 10 sts on opposite side of instep, P across 13 sts from st holder (57 sts on needle). Work in stockinette st for 1 inch. **NEXT ROW**: K 2 tog, K 22, K 2 tog, K 5, sl 1, K 1, p.s.s.o., K 22, K 2 tog. **NEXT ROW**: P across dec 1 st at each end of row. **NEXT ROW**: K 2 tog, K 19, K 2 tog, K 5, sl 1, K 1, p.s.s.o., K 19, K 2 tog. **NEXT ROW**: P across dec 1 st at each end of row. **NEXT ROW**: K 2 tog, K 19, K 2 tog, K 5, sl 1, K 1, p.s.s.o., K 19, K 2 tog. **NEXT ROW**: P across dec 1 st at each end of row. Bind off. Sew sole and back seam. Lace ribbon through beading.

MITTENS

Cast on 41 sts. Work in seed st for 8 rows. **NEXT ROW**: P across. **NEXT ROW**: Work beading same as booties. Work in stockinette until mitten measures 3¾ inches from beg ending with a P row. **NEXT ROW**: K 1, * K 2 tog, repeat from * across row. **NEXT ROW**: P across. Repeat last 2 rows once, cut yarn leaving an 8 inch length. Thread yarn into needle and draw through remaining sts. Fasten securely and sew seam. Lace ribbon through beading.

HAT

Cast on 85 sts. Work in K 1, P 1 ribbing for 1½ inches. Then work in seed st for 1½ inches. * Work 8 rows stockinette. Work 8 rows seed st. Repeat from * twice, cut yarn leaving about a 10 inch length. Thread into needle and draw yarn through all sts. Sew back seam. Turn ribbing to inside of hat and sew in position. **POMPON**: Wind yarn 100 times over a 2 inch cardboard. Slip off cardboard. Tie in center and cut each end. Attach pompon to top of hat. Finish with rosettes and ribbon as illustrated.

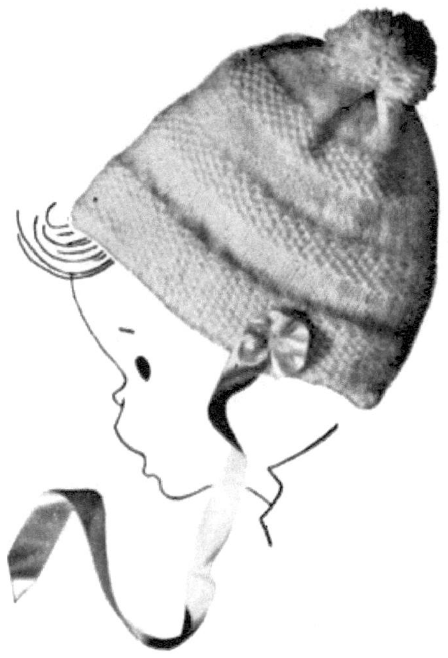

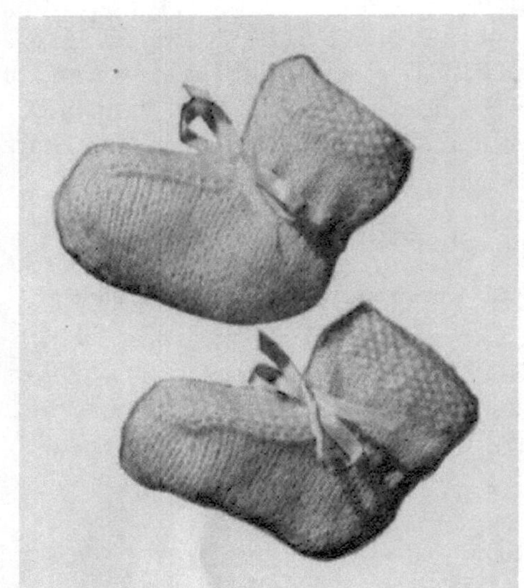

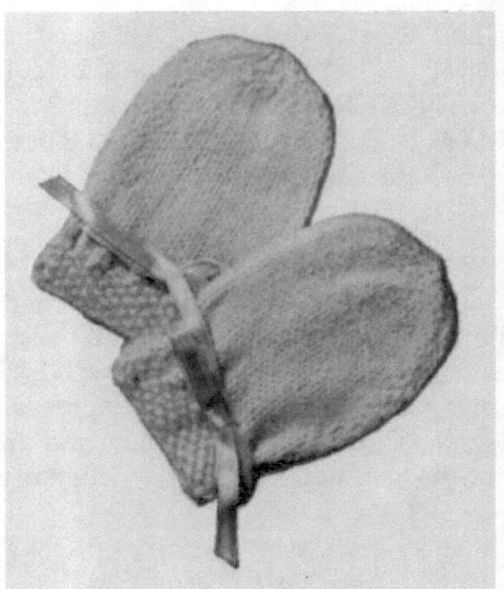

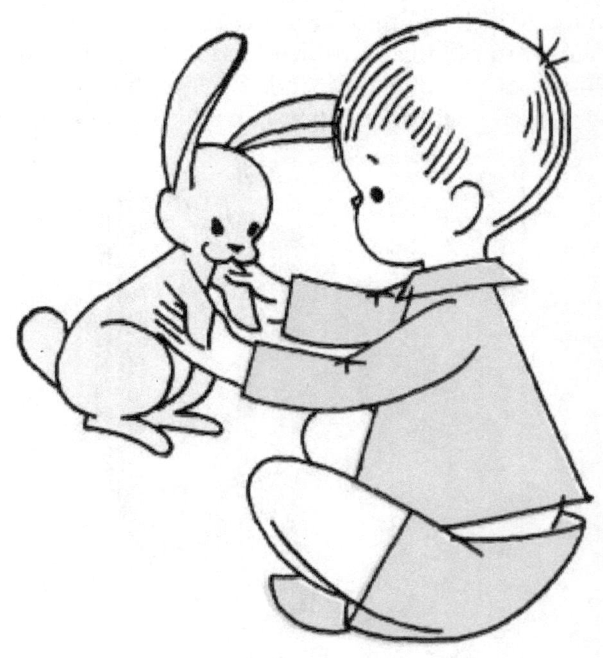

HAPPY SWEATER DATES

HIS SLIPOVER SIZES: 40, 42 AND 44

Materials Required:

AMERICAN THREAD COMPANY "DAWN" KNITTING WORSTED 6 (6, 7) 4 ounce skeins Cinnamon or Red

1 Pr. Knitting Needles No. 8 and No. 10 OR ANY SIZE NEEDLES WHICH WILL RESULT IN STITCH GAUGE BELOW.

GAUGE for No. 10 Needles: 9 sts = 2 inches

Directions are given for size 40. Changes for sizes 42 and 44 are given in parentheses.

BACK: On No. 8 needles cast on 92 (96, 100) sts. Work in K 2, P 2 ribbing for 1½ inches inc 1 st on last row of ribbing (all sizes). Change to No. 10 needles. **START PATTERN: 1st ROW**: K across row. **2nd ROW**: K 1, * yarn to front, sl 1, yarn to back, K 1, repeat from * across row. Repeat 1st and 2nd rows 3 times. **9th ROW**: K across row. **10th ROW**: K 2, * yarn to front, sl 1, yarn to back, K 1, repeat from * across row ending last repeat with K 2. Repeat 9th and 10th rows 3 times. Repeat from 1st pattern row until back measures 15 (15½, 16) inches from beg. **SHAPE ARMHOLES**: Bind off 5 sts at beg of next 2 rows (all sizes); then dec 1 st at each end every other row 3 times. Work even until armholes measure 9 (9½, 10) inches.

SHAPE SHOULDERS: Bind off 8 sts at beg of next 4 rows (all sizes). **NEXT ROW: NECK FACING**: P across row. Then work in stockinette st (P 1 row, K 1 row) for 5 rows inc 1 st at beg and end of every row. Bind off.

FRONT: Work same as back.

SLEEVES: On No. 8 needles cast on 48 (50, 52) sts and work in K 2, P 2 ribbing (all sizes) for 1½ inches inc 1 st in last row of ribbing (all sizes). Change to No. 10 needles and keeping pattern as established inc 1 st at beg and end of every 10th row until there are 71 (73, 75) sts on needle. Work even until sleeve measures 19 (19¼, 19½) inches from beg or length desired to underarm. **SHAPE SLEEVE**: Bind off 5 sts at beg of next 2 rows; then dec 1 st at beg and end of every other row until there are 33 (33, 35) sts; then bind off 3 sts at beg of next 4 rows. Bind off remaining sts.

FINISHING: Block each section. Sew shoulder, side and sleeve seams. Sew sleeves in position. Fold neck facing to inside of sweater and tack in position.

HER RAGLAN SIZES: SMALL, MEDIUM AND LARGE

Materials Required:

AMERICAN THREAD COMPANY "DAWN" KNITTING WORSTED 5 (5, 6) 4 ounce skeins Watermelon

1 Pr. Knitting Needles No. 8 OR ANY SIZE NEEDLES WHICH WILL RESULT IN STITCH GAUGE BELOW.

1 Set of Double Pointed Knitting Needles No. 8.

GAUGE:. 9 sts = 2 inches;
6 rows = 1 inch

Directions are given for small size. Changes for medium and large sizes given in parentheses.

BACK: Cast on 76 (80, 84) sts. **1st and 2nd ROWS**: K 2, P 2 across each row. **3rd and 4th ROWS**: P 2, K 2 across each row. Repeat last 4 rows for 12 (12½, 13) inches or length desired to underarm. **SHAPE RAGLAN**: Dec 1 st at beg of each row until 24 sts remain (all sizes), slip 24 sts to st holder.

FRONT: Work same as back.

SLEEVES: Cast on 32 (36, 40) sts. Work in pattern for 3 inches inc 1 st each side every inch 13 times working inc sts into established pattern, 58 (62, 66) sts. Work even until sleeve measures 17 inches or length desired to underarm. **SHAPE RAGLAN**: Work same as back until 8 sts remain. Work 1 row even (all sizes). Sl 8 sts to st holder.

FINISHING: Steam each section lightly. Sew side and sleeve seams. Sew sleeves in position. Dividing sts evenly, sl all sts from stitch holders to 3 double pointed needles and work in pattern for 2 inches; then K each row for 2 inches for neck facing. Bind off loosely. Turn neck facing to inside and sew in place.

SINGLE CROCHET: (s c) Insert hook in row or st, pick up yarn, pull through, yarn over and pull through the 2 loops on hook.

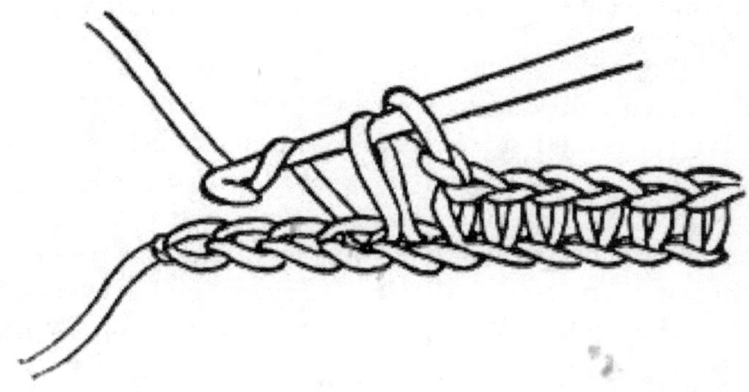

SLIP STITCH: (sl st) Insert hook in st, pick up yarn and pull through loop on hook.

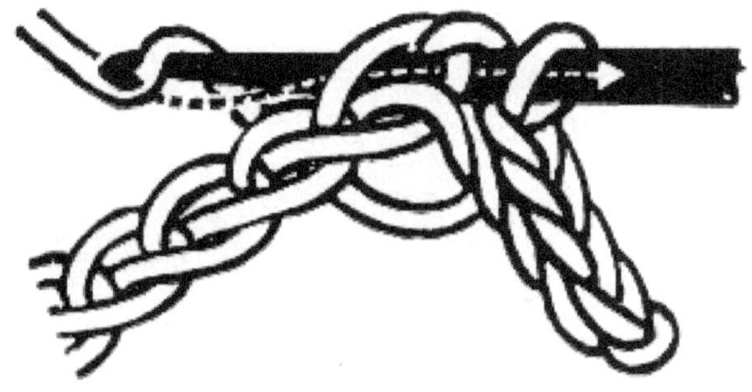

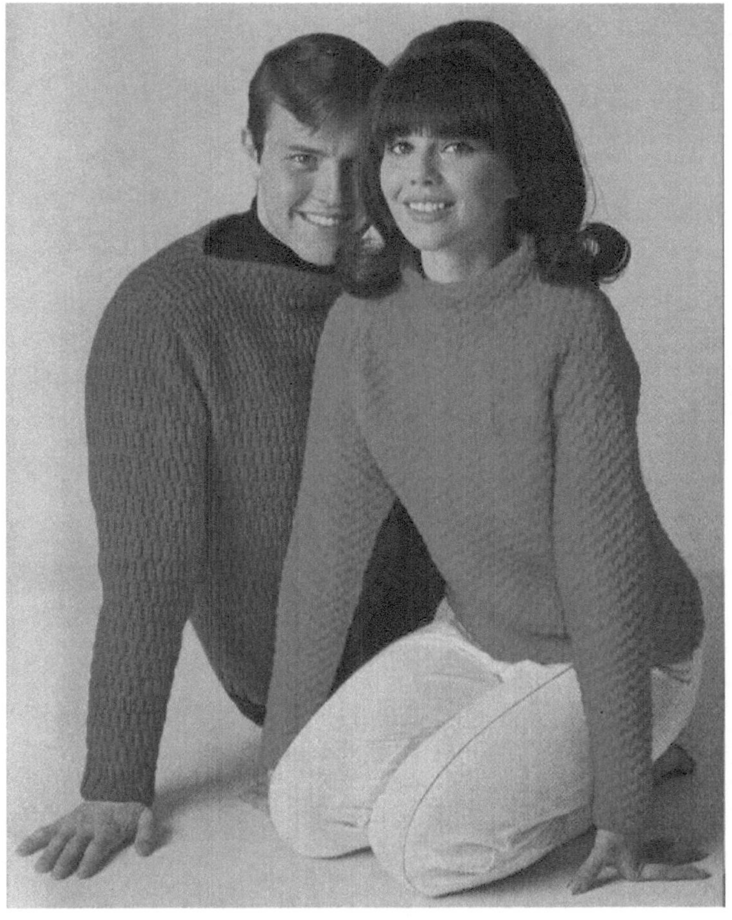

BASIC CROCHET

CLAM DIGGERS SHELL

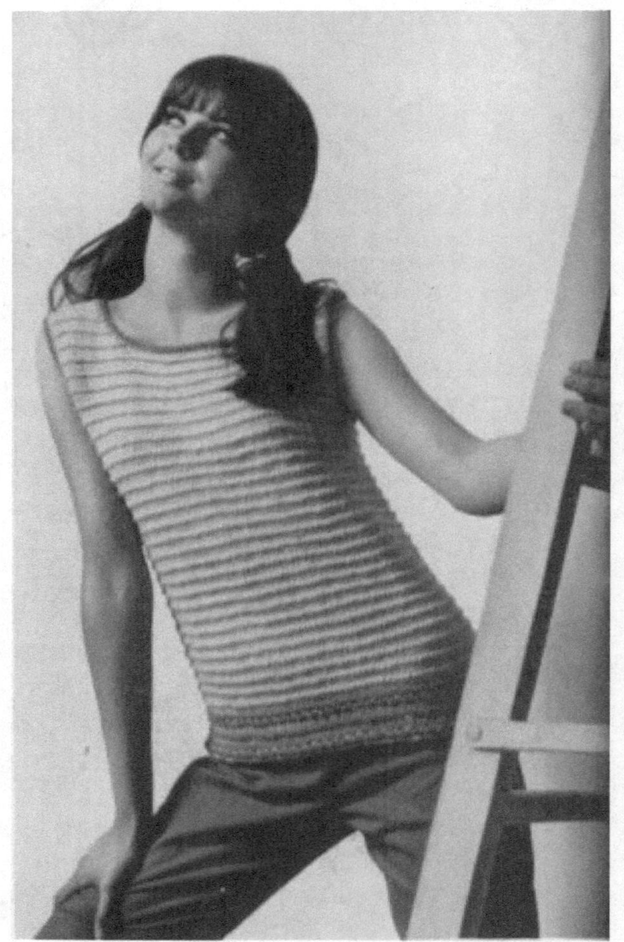

SIZES: SMALL, MEDIUM, LARGE

Materials Required:

AMERICAN THREAD COMPANY "DAWN" KNITTING WORSTED

3 (3, 4) 4 ounce skeins Canary

1—4 ounce skein Tangerine

1 Pr. Knitting Needles No. 9 OR ANY SIZE NEEDLES WHICH WILL RESULT IN STITCH GAUGE BELOW.

Plastic Crochet Hook Size H

GAUGE: 9 sts = 2 inches

Directions are given for small size. Changes for medium and large sizes are given in parentheses.

BACK: With Canary (Main Color) cast on 73 (77, 81) sts. **1st ROW**: P across row. **2nd ROW**: K across row, drop MC. **3rd and 4th ROWS**: With Tangerine (Contrasting Color) K across each row, drop CC. **5th ROW**: With MC, K 1, * yarn to back sl 1 as if to P, K 1, repeat from * across row. **6th ROW**: K 1, * yarn to front, sl 1 as if to P, K 1 repeat from * across row, drop MC. **7th and 8th ROWS**: With CC K across each row, drop CC. **9th ROW**: With MC K across row. **10th ROW**: P across row, drop MC. **11th and 12th ROWS**: With CC K across each row, drop CC. **13th ROW**: With MC K across row. **14th ROW**: P across row, drop MC. **15th and 16th ROWS**: With CC K across each row, drop CC. **17th ROW**: With MC repeat 5th row. **18th ROW**: Repeat 6th row. **19th and 20th ROWS**: With CC K across each row, drop CC. **21st ROW**: With MC K across row. **22nd ROW**: P across row. With MC repeat from 19th to 22nd rows for pattern. Work even in pattern until back measures 13½ inches from beg or desired length to underarm. **SHAPE ARMHOLES**: Bind off 3 (4, 5) sts at beg of next 2 rows; then dec 1 st at each end every other row 4 times. Work even on 59 (61, 63) sts until armholes measure 7 (7¼, 7½) inches from 1st bind off. Work across 12 (13, 14) sts, bind off next 35 sts for back of neck, work across remaining sts. **NEXT ROW**: Tie in another skein of yarn and working both sides at same time dec 1 st at each side of neck edge. **NEXT ROW**: Work even. **NEXT ROW**: Dec 1 st at each side of neck edge. **NEXT 2 ROWS**. **SHAPE SHOULDERS**: Bind off 5 (5, 6) sts at beg of each row, bind off 5 (6, 6) sts at beg of next 2 rows.

FRONT: Work same as back to underarm, Shape Armholes same as back. Work even until armholes measure 4½ (4¾, 5) inches.

SHAPE NECK: Work across 17 (18, 19) sts, bind off next 25 sts, work across remaining sts. **NEXT ROW**: Tie in another skein of yarn and working both sides at same time dec 1 st at each side of neck edge, then dec 1 st at each side of neck edge every other row 6 more times. Work even until armholes measure same as back. Shape Shoulders same as back.

FINISHING: Block each section. Sew shoulder and side seams matching patterns. **NECK EDGE**: Attach MC at left shoulder and work a row of s c all around neck edge working 1 s c in every other row on sides, 1 s c in each bound off st across front and back, join, cut MC. Attach CC and work 1 s c in each st, join, cut yarn. **ARMHOLE EDGE**: Attach MC at underarm and work 1 s c in each bound off st at underarm and 1 s c in every other row around armhole, join, cut yarn. **NEXT ROW**: Attach CC and work 1 s c in each s c, join, cut yarn.

POM PON PONCHO

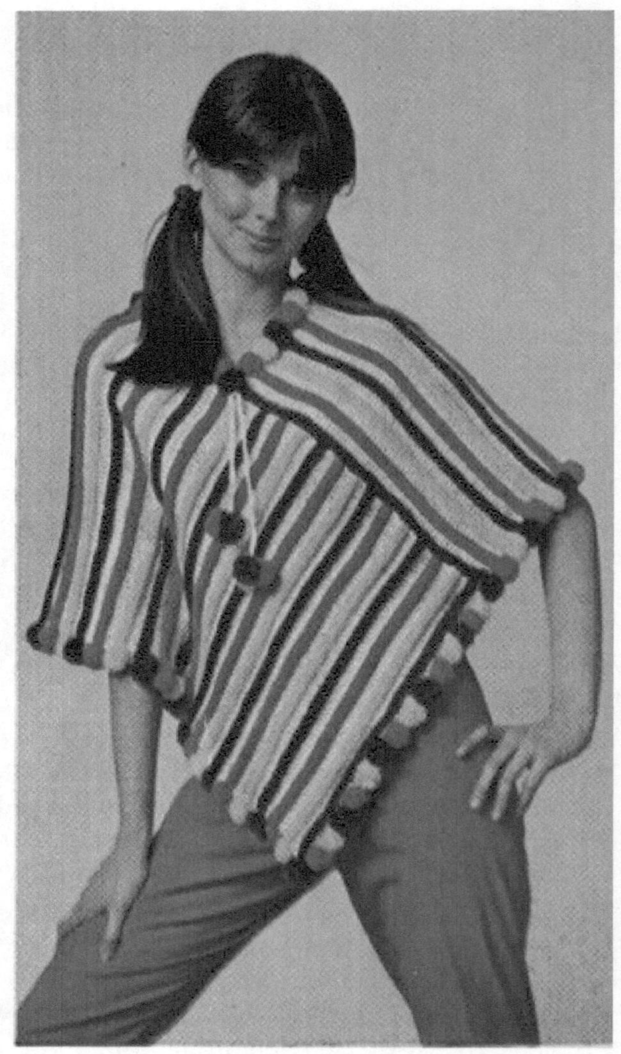

SIZE: ONE SIZE FITS ALL

Materials Required:

AMERICAN THREAD COMPANY "DAWN" KNITTING WORSTED

2—4 ounce Skeins White

1—4 ounce Skein each Olive Green, Canary and Watermelon.

1 Pr. Knitting Needles No. 8 OR ANY SIZE NEEDLES WHICH WILL RESULT IN STITCH GAUGE BELOW.

Plastic Crochet Hook Size G

GAUGE: 9 sts = 2 inches

With Olive Green cast on 63 sts. **1st ROW:** K. **2nd ROW:** P. **3rd ROW:** K, drop Olive Green. **4th ROW:** With White K. **5th ROW:** P. **6th ROW:** K. **7th ROW:** P, drop White. **8th ROW:** With Watermelon K. **9th ROW:** K. **10th ROW:** P. **11th ROW:** K, drop Watermelon. **12th ROW:** With White K. **13th ROW:** P. **14th ROW:** K. **15th ROW:** P, drop White. **16th ROW:** With Canary K. **17th ROW:** K. **18th ROW:** P. **19th ROW:** K, drop Canary. **20th ROW:** With White K. **21st ROW:** P. **22nd ROW:** K. **23rd ROW:** P, drop White. **24th ROW:** With Olive Green K. Repeat from 1st row until there are 28 colored stripes (10 Olive Green). Bind off.

Work a 2nd section in same manner.

FINISHING: Working down 1 long side attach White in 1st st of Olive Green stripe; with crochet hook work 4 s c in each White stripe down side skipping all colored stripes to corner working the s c over all ends of carried colors. Working across short end, work 1 s c in each st, cut yarn. Complete other section in same manner. Block to measure 14 × 28 inches.

Sew one short unfinished end to one long unfinished side sewing to within the center of 14th White stripe. Finish other side in same manner. This leaves 14 stripes on each section free for neck opening. Attach White at neck opening and work 4 s c over each White stripe, join. **NEXT ROW:** Work a sl st in each st, join cut yarn. With White work an 18 inch ch. Attach to center of neck. Finish ends with 3 pompons as illustrated.

POMPONS: Wind yarn 14 times over 2 legs of a chair or any open flat surface (28 strands). Tie with a 6 inch strand at 1¼ inch intervals, cut between ties. Attach a pompon of matching color to each stripe alternating colors across each Olive Green stripe.

PRETEEN SLIPOVER

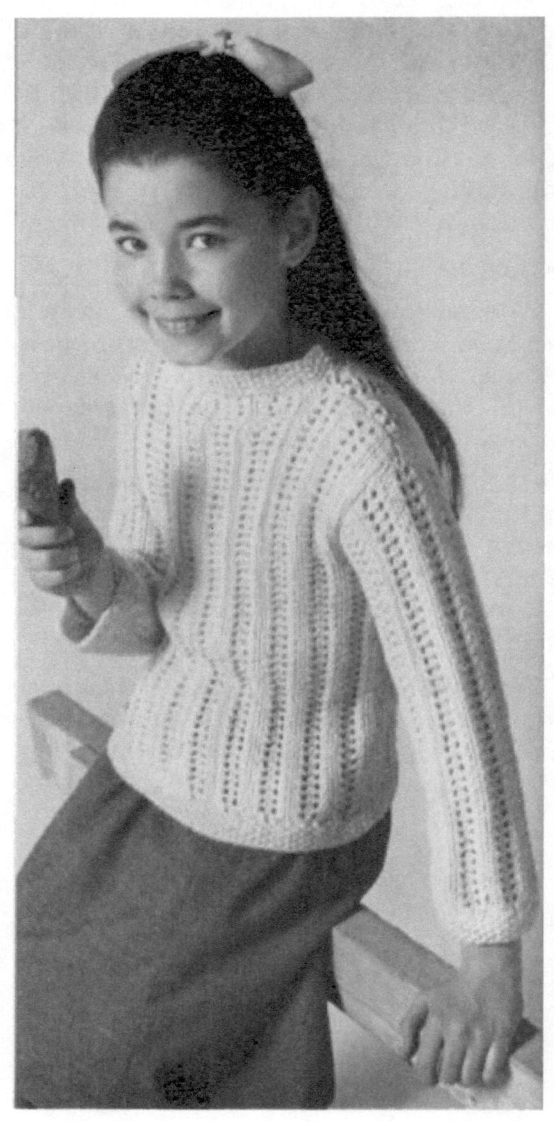

SIZES 4, 6, 8, 10, 12, 14

Materials Required:

AMERICAN THREAD COMPANY "DAWN" KNITTING WORSTED 2 (3, 3, 3, 3, 4) 4 ounce skeins Canary

1 Pr. Knitting Needles No. 8 OR ANY SIZE NEEDLES WHICH WILL RESULT IN STITCH GAUGE BELOW.

GAUGE: 5 sts = 1 inch

Directions are given for size 4. Changes for sizes 6, 8, 10, 12 and 14 are given in parentheses.

BACK: Cast on 53 (59, 65, 71, 77, 83) sts. Work in seed st for 1 inch (seed st: * K 1, P 1, repeat from * across row ending with K 1). **START PATTERN** as follows: **1st ROW**: K 5, * P 1, K 5, repeat from * across row. **2nd ROW**: P 5, * K 1, P 5, repeat from * across row. **3rd ROW**: K 3, * K 2 tog, Y O, P 1, Y O, K 2 tog through back of sts, K 1, repeat from * across row ending with K 2 more sts. **4th ROW**: P 5, * K 1, P 5, repeat from across row. Repeat 3rd and 4th rows for pattern. Work even in pattern until work measures 9 (10, 11, 11½, 12, 12½) inches from beg. **SHAPE ARM-HOLES: Next 2 ROWS**: Bind off 6 sts at beg of each row (all sizes) Work even in pattern until armhole measures 4½ (5, 5½, 6, 7, 7) inches. **SHAPE SHOULDERS**: Bind off 6 sts at beg of next 4 rows (all sizes), bind off remaining 17 (23, 29, 35, 41, 47) sts.

FRONT: Work same as back.

SLEEVES: Cast on 31 (31, 37, 43, 49, 49) sts. Work in seed st pattern for 1 inch inc 10 sts on last row (all sizes). Work even in pattern until sleeves measure 12 (12½, 13½, 14½, 16, 16) inches from beg, bind off all sts.

FINISHING: Block each section. Sew one shoulder seam. With wrong side of work facing, pick up and K each st at neck edge across front and back. Work in seed st pattern for 1 inch (all sizes), bind off in pattern. Sew opposite shoulder and side of collar. Sew side seams. Sew sleeve seams sewing seams to within 1 inch less than length at armhole edge. Sew sleeves in position sewing the 1 inch at underarm to bound off sts.

Lector House believes that a society develops through a two-fold approach of continuous learning and adaptation, which is derived from the study of classic literary works spread across the historic timeline of literature records. Therefore, we aim at reviving, repairing and redeveloping all those inaccessible or damaged but historically as well as culturally important literature across subjects so that the future generations may have an opportunity to study and learn from past works to embark upon a journey of creating a better future.

This book is a result of an effort made by Lector House towards making a contribution to the preservation and repair of original ancient works which might hold historical significance to the approach of continuous learning across subjects.

HAPPY READING & LEARNING!

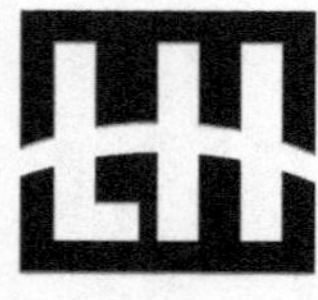

LECTOR HOUSE LLP
E-MAIL: lectorpublishing@gmail.com